How to Sell You
Spai

(even in a Recession)

By Felix Joseph

www.howtosellyourpropertyinspain.com

www.howtobuyapropertyinspain.com

www.webuyhousesspain.com

www.puor.co.uk

ABOUT

This is a book to help you to sell your property in Spain. Most of the time, I will address your property as your home but be clear I am talking about your house, flat, apartment, villa, Finca, or any other form of residential property you own and would like to sell quickly and for the best price possible.

I am currently based in Andalucía in Spain, and so this book has been written for my immediate markets, who are indigenous and overseas owners of Spanish property who want or need to sell it even if the property market is in decline. As such, in terms of terminology, I discuss prices in Euros; my advice regarding the selling process relates to the Spanish selling process, and the information on taxes and legality are written so that it is correct as applied only to the laws which govern Spain.

That said, even if you do not own a property in Spain, as long as you have a property to sell, this book will still be of invaluable use to you. Most of the advice in this book applies to selling a property anywhere in the world. Certainly, some aspects such as the legal system, sales commissions, and selling costs will differ, as will some of the norms surrounding access to the MLS system or agreements with estate agents, but the core principles, strategy, and approach of this book need only a slight adjustment to apply to selling any property anywhere in the world.

The aspects of this book that are universal are the aspects such as the traditional methods of marketing your property, the viewing process, sales training, and tips on property sales negotiation. These aspects, along with your sales plan, house doctoring, and digital marketing, are all things that can be used to sell any property anywhere.

I have been in the property game for over twenty years as an investor, real estate agent, property consultant, and portfolio builder, so I am writing from experience. Some of my ideas and suggestions may be controversial, but I promise you that they are not made for controversies' sake. Everything written in this book has been tried and tested and proven to help me sell properties not only from my own portfolio but properties owned by my many clients over the years

But as with all information, my suggestion to you is to use what resonates with you, and you feel comfortable doing and let the suggestions and recommendations which you are uncomfortable with you to pass you buy.

Either way, whatever you use or do not use from this book, I know that it will help you to get your property sold quickly and for the best price possible even in the worst economic circumstances, and to that end, I wish you good luck

FORWARD: YOU CAN'T MOW YOUR OWN LAWN.

You can't mow your own lawn, or to put it more succinctly (unless you are a landscape gardener), you really shouldn't. This is one of the most important business lessons for any entrepreneur, sole trader, and SME owner. In fact, it is a lesson that even some CEOs of big corporations need to learn. You can't mow your own lawn is effectively a modern-day twist on time is money.

So time is money, yes, we all know that, and by now, most of us understand that in its essence, this means that you can either throw time at solving a problem or money at solving a problem. Throwing time at solving a problem reminds me of a story boastfully told to me by an ex-property associate of mine. He told me that his wife had told him that she wanted a new Kitchen, so he called a few kitchen fitters for a quote. Upon hearing the quote, he exclaimed, 'How much!!!!!, I'm not paying that' and so pledged to do it himself. He then went on to state with the kind of boastful pride that should have alerted me to his sociopathy much earlier, 'And I did fit it, it took me five years in all, but I did fit that kitchen.' That is throwing time at a problem, whereas unless you simply could not afford it or you personally enjoy kitchen fitting and use the process as part of your leisure time, the rest of us would merely find a quote that we were happy with, employ the professional and have the kitchen completed before our family starved to death or developed obesity from 5 years worth of take-out food. That is throwing money at a problem.

If your house hasn't sold, it's a problem; the more positively minded self-improvement guru types amongst you might decide that you would prefer to use the word challenge. The point I'm making is that this problem or challenge needs results, and the quickest way to get those results is to throw money at selling it.

In fact, the quickest way to almost get any result in the western world is to throw money at it. Don't believe me? Let me explain. You can spend hours and hours and a few hours more watching YouTube videos trying to find the right free online fitness trainer who has the right training regime and nutritional program which fits your exact body type and metabolism, or you can just spend the money to find yourself a personal trainer who creates a training, eating and nutritional regime which is 100% tailored specifically for you. It costs you a lot more money, but I will stake my life on the fact that you will get the results you want in a much shorter time.

This is why this is not strictly a 'for sale by owner' book (also known as FSBO). Sure, selling your property FSBO will save you the cost of paying the real estate agent their commission for the sale, or to put it another way, selling with an estate agent will cost you more money to sell your property (throwing money at the problem). But being limited to selling your property yourself may increase the time it takes for it to sell and may lead you to have to sell it for less. What we will promote in this book is a blended process of selling your property yourself (FSBO) whilst also having it listed with the best local estate agents at a commission structure that suits you. The aim is to give you the best of all worlds by teaching you to market and sell the property yourself so that you can try to sell your property commission-free in the first instance, but also provide you with the safety net of getting your property sold quickly by throwing money at it and paying estate agents their commission if they manage to sell it before you can.

Let me explain in more detail why we promote using both real estate agents and FSBO in this book. Firstly, because if you do not give a real estate agent an 'exclusive listing,' then in most cases, it will not cost you anything to list your property with them. You are effectively giving her the chance to earn a commission by selling it, so let her run around and promote it in an attempt to earn her money. In this book, you will find sections on how to choose the best estate agent to list your property and how to get the best deal from them when you find one by leveraging the fact that they all use the Multi Listings System, also known as the MLS.

If you use all of the tips, tricks and strategies suggested in this book, then there will be no upfront costs or losses in the use of a real estate agent. But if they do sell the property for you, it will save you time in selling the property, and as I will demonstrate later in this book, when selling a property, time is very much literally money. Also, the money you throw at the sale is not money you pay upfront; it's money that you pay upon the completion of the sale, so unless they actually find a buyer for your property, in most cases listing it for sale with them costs you nothing. If they do find a buyer for your property, then you will have to pay them (do not even think about trying to sideline them and going directly to the buyer they found because they will sue you for their commission plus expenses and, quite rightly too). Do not begrudge them their money because if your property has sold, they have earned it.

The only exception to this two-pronged selling technique we recommend is if you genuinely cannot afford to pay the real estate commission when you sell your property. Here in Spain, real estate commissions are quite high, between 5% and 7%, depending on the real estate agent you use, so you are going to have to make sure that you can afford to pay that 5% in addition to all of the other costs of sale and any debts which you will need to pay when you sell your property. Make sure that you've done your budget and you can afford to give that 5% of the sales price away to them for their work in finding you a buyer and getting the sale done quickly.

If you're not in a position to spend that money, for example, if the debts against the property are so high that based on the true market value you can't afford to pay a real estate agent and clear all of the debts, then get in contact with a company like ours who can help you with a negotiated debt reduction or a creative sales strategy to allow you to get the property sold. Failing this, you are going to be restricted to the 'for sale by owner' model, but don't worry; there is more than enough information in this book for you to complete your sale using this method successfully as FSBO methodology and practicality is one of the major things that this book is here to help   you   with

CHAPTERS

CHAPTER 1: IT'S YOUR RESPONSIBILITY

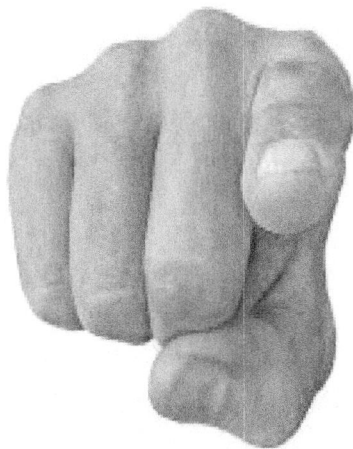

It's your responsibility

With great power comes great responsibility. In terms of your personal economics, your property is probably your greatest financial asset and, if managed correctly, held on to for a business cycle or two and then sold with good timing; property wields the greatest amount of financial power most of us will ever have. Creating this kind of financial power for myself is what got me into property investment in the first place, and helping others to access it is why I set up businesses in the property space and continue to work there

But with this huge potential financial power comes an even bigger financial responsibility which is managing, maintaining, possibly renting, and eventually selling your property. Make no mistake, just as the spoils from the financial success are yours, so are the problems, frustrations, and hard work associated with the responsibility.

Over my many years working with property investors, I have developed a realisation, 'When I find a client a deal which makes them money, they tell everyone how clever they were for buying it; if the market changes and it creates any difficulty for them, they tell everyone it was my fault for selling it to them.'

Don't be this person. If you are responsible for the success, you are also responsible for the failure, and if you want to be responsible for the profits, you need to be responsible for the sale ultimately.

So do not adopt the attitude that it's your real estate agent's job to sell your property. This will create the wrong attitude within yourself and cause you to leave it looking like a mess, not do essential repairs, not play your part in sales negotiations, not be available for viewings, and not be involved in the advertising. Also, if you adopt this attitude, you will put yourself in the position of being 'just another one of his clients', and that is not the place you want to be. You want to be his number one client with the property he is trying his hardest to sell.

If you need to sell your property, especially if you're competing with everyone else trying to sell in the middle of a recession, it is not your estate agent's responsibility to sell your property. It is his job to sell your property, but it not his responsibility. It's your responsibility to sell your property.

It's your responsibility to sell your property, and common sense should tell you that you should help everybody involved in the process of selling your property as much as possible in order to get the job done as quickly and profitably as possible.

He might get a commission, but you will get the profit as well as the other benefits such as stress reduction and freedom from the ongoing running costs such as government taxes and community fees. Freedom in terms of your ability to move location, re-invest the deposit you paid as a down payment or your profits from the sale, and all the other things that you want and are the reason you're selling in the first place.

So don't get it twisted, the sale of your home is your responsibility, and this book aims to walk you through this responsibility and help you to discharge it effectively.

Your estate agent, like anybody else in business, wants to make money. If he sees that you are proactive in helping him do his job to sell your property, he will move you up his priority scale.

Why? Because your help is going to allow him to sell your property quickly, therefore helping him to make money more quickly and easily which is good for his business. This is the person you want to be in his eyes, not the person who either willingly or unbeknown makes his job of selling his property more difficult by leaving it messy, not tidying it up, refusing to negotiate, or not assisting by being available for viewings. These people go down the scale of importance in the real estate agents list.

So regardless of the fact that it's his job to sell your property, he still has to want to do it. He still has to make a business decision as to which clients he works for first and which clients he works for the hardest. This isn't him being malicious. This is strictly a business decision based on your behaviour and its probability to create a scenario that leads to success for both of you. So you need to make sure that you are the person, you are the seller, and you are the client for whom it makes good business sense for him to put his time and effort behind.

Why do you want to sell?

There is a psychology behind sales (in fact, there is a psychology behind everything we do, and to put it simply, the more in touch with why we want to achieve anything, the more likely we are to get it). What this means to you is that you not only need to know that you want to sell your property; you actually need to know why.

Make a list of the reasons you want to sell your property, all of them. If your only reason is 'to get the money,' this is not a list at all. If you have completed your list and there are less than ten reasons, then go back to it and add to it. No course of action taken has only one or two reasons behind it, and it is by exploring all of the reasons that you want to achieve a goal, big and small, important and less important, that you will find the hidden information which you will need to guide you on exactly how to achieve that goal to your satisfaction.

I have read a lot of 'How to sell your property books,' and again, this is something I never see. I might be the only person giving this advice, but trust me, it is sound, and you would do well to take it.

Knowing why you want to sell, I mean why you really want to sell, is super essential. A good real estate agent will try and elicit some of this information from you, but nobody will make this list as comprehensive as you. And more importantly, nobody is going to be able to drill down into the real reasons and the real value of you selling your property than you yourself. So this is essential, it is non-negotiable, and you will understand why it is when we come into the negotiation section.

So when making that list of why you want to sell, the obvious answer is that you want the money. Ok, check, but not enough. We need a list of a minimum of ten and preferably twenty reasons, yes, twenty separate reasons (even if some are related) as to why you want to sell the property.

Let me give you a few examples of how to do this.

Why do I want to sell my property? Well, I want the money. Ok, but what do I want to do with this money? This is what really lies behind the first answer. Ask yourself why you want the money; what are you going to do with it? What are you going to spend it on? How will it make you feel to have the security of it in the bank? How will you feel if you can use it to lend to others in need? Ask yourself these types of questions at least three to five times, and this will start to elicit some of the other answers or the deeper reasons you want to sell.

So let's try it again. Why are you selling the property? Is it because you want the money? Ok then, why do you want the money? List five things that you are going to spend it on

Next question, why do you want the money rather than the property? I mean, when you bought the property, you wanted the property more than the money you spent on it, so what's changed? Potential answers could be that; you are no longer going to visit Spain. You are getting a bit old for a holiday home. External circumstances (such as Brexit or the Covid 19 Pandemic) has made ownership a different proposition than it was when you first bought the property, and so on. List every reason the money is now more important to you than continuing to own the property itself.

Here are some more examples of questions to ask yourself and possible answers.

Could you use that money elsewhere? Could you use that money to do things in your country of birth, the country where you live, or another territory? And if so, Why? What things do you want to do there?

Do you have other or newer commitments that are now more important than owning the property? Do you have grandchildren that you want to relocate to spend more time with? Maybe you want to help to get your children or grandchildren to get on the property ladder? Or could you pay down some of your UK debt?

Do you no longer think that the money is doing well for you invested in the property in Spain? Maybe you could pull it out of Spain and re-invest it in another place or asset class for the future.

Keep asking yourself questions upon questions. The process should go like this:

Another reason I want to sell is

'Well, I don't really use it anymore.'

Why?

'Because of the changes in travel due to Covid and Brexit.'

How will those changes affect your use of the property?

'Well, I don't think I'll be taking as many foreign holidays in the future.'

Why?

Because I can't be bothered with the extra hassle.'

So?

'So the property is going to stay there empty unless I can get it rented.'

Well, why don't you just rent it out?

'Well, I have had rental properties before, and it did not suit my personality, so I know that I do not want to be a landlord again....'

And here's an example for a property bought as an investment property for rental, just for good measure

Why do I want to sell?

'Because I'm not getting as many rentals as I used to.'

Why is that?

'Well, because my market was primarily the Brits staying for 6-month rentals and fewer Brits are now going to my part of Spain'

What has caused the change?

'Because of new regulations created by Brexit, they can no longer stay in Spain for the same lengths of time, in the same numbers or in the same way.'

Why?

'Because of the changes such as the need for Visas and time restrictions caused by the new regulations as a result of the change in status of Brits going from EU members to non-EU members and the additional hassles and problems this has caused for UK overseas travel.'

Any other reasons?

'Yes, many people have got used to taking staycations because of COVID, they have rediscovered holidaying in the UK and are now choosing to do so to avoid the extra effort, and annoyance overseas travel now requires.'

Please note that these questions and answers are only examples of the kind of conversations that may or may not be going on in your head. The point here is to ask yourself the questions and really drill down into the reasons behind them in order to be 100% clear of every benefit that you perceive you will get from the sale and every pain or problem you will relieve yourself from once you have it sold.

Once you have your ten solid reasons (twenty for the overachievers in the group), this is going to be your basis for what you choose to accept or refuse in negotiation. You see, a truism often overlooked is that price is simply a measure of value. That is why this exercise is a must because it allows you to really discover the value of selling the property to you. What it means not only to your finances but also to your health, relationships with family members, peace of mind, and every aspect of your life. That is the true value that you receive when you sell a property, and as such, this is the information you need to know and have clearly in your mind before you set a price or enter into a price negotiation

To further explain this principle, here is a simple example.

You bought the property for 50,000 well over a property cycle ago, so you have priced it at 100,000, which is in line with other similar properties on the market at the moment. Amongst the property viewers, somebody offers you 80,000 euros for the property, that's 20,000 below what you wanted. The ego says no, you know a property sold for 95,000 the other day, and you don't even think it was as good as yours. So you refuse the offer. This is what most people do. This is an action taken from the view of only taking money into account in terms of the value that the sale represents. It is the ego's view and not the view that would have been taken if you included the big picture.

Ok, so let's look at the big picture.

Why do you want to sell it?

'Well, property prices are currently at an all-time high, and you think that there may be a property crash around the corner.'

Ok then, why is that important?

'Well, you think that the value of your property is going to drop by 30%, possibly in the next year or so.'

Okay, and what will that mean to you?

'Well, if you don't sell the property in the next twelve to eighteen months, you believe that you will probably be lucky to get 70,000 for it if you can sell it at all.'

Why will not selling in the next eighteen months be a problem?

'Well, asides from the potential loss of profit, you really need that money to invest in your family. Your Son is finishing his dental degree at the end of the year, and you promised to invest in him so that he can set up his own surgery. So if you do not sell before prices fall, you will not be able to keep to your commitment.'

And why is this important

'Well, you only originally bought the property as a way of investing for your family because you knew that over time, property usually outperformed shares and government bonds, so it is really important that you have the money out of this investment in time for when your family needs it.

Now just based on this information alone, the 80,000 offer now becomes more feasible. Should you take the 80,000 offer straight away? No, that's what negotiations are for. What you need to do is counteroffer or maybe increase the value of your property offering and see how far up you can push the buyer. You may well find that because they know that the 80,000 euros is a cheeky offer, they will settle with you for nearer to 90,000.

Now, based on your reasons why, the real reasons that you are selling the property, the things that your self-questioning has taught you. You know that an 80,000 offer actually would have been acceptable, and as such, the buyers' final offer of 87,000 offers now seems a lot better than it would have if you adjust based on your calculation of getting 100% on your original asking price.

You only get to this kind of understanding if you have a clear sense of why you want to sell and the impact that everything associated with selling the property will have on your life. It allows you to ask questions such as;

Do you really want to hold out for 5,000 pounds more and risk not being able to help your grandchildren get on the property ladder?

Do you really want to stubbornly hold out for 3,000 euros more, causing you to lose the sale only to be forced to sell for 15,000 euros less than you refused a mere six months later in a property crash that you yourself predicted?

Do you really want to hold out for 10,000 euros more and miss the opportunity to buy your dream home in the UK, the place that you intend to relocate to, which is the only reason you need the money from your Spanish property sale in the first place?

Or miss the opportunity to invest in the massive uplift in Bitcoin that you know is about to happen because you have been studying the market, and you know that another 'Bitcoin to the moon' run is around the corner. Do you really want to miss out on this by holding out for your asking price even though this reinvestment of the money from the property sales will be worth ten times more than the amount you reduced the price of your property to sell?

If you're so busy caught up in the minutia of the property sales price that your ego tells you not to sell at a discount, you may earn 5,000 pounds more on the sale but miss out on 30,000 pounds on an alternative investment.

(Disclaimer: these are all fictitious examples, and nothing herein constitutes advice of imminent property price crashes or, more importantly, Bitcoin going to the moon, but hopefully, they will help you to get the picture of how knowing the real reasons you want to sell and will help you to assess offers in terms of their real value to you)

Whatever your bag is, whatever your reasons, you need the full picture in order to appreciate and work on the value of what's being offered to you in a sales negotiation.

Knowing the real reasons you want to sell allows you to see the value of what the buyer is offering you when he makes an offer to buy, just as much as knowing your property allows you to tell the buyer the full value of what you're offering him when you make a counteroffer.

We will spend a lot of time on this book focused on your ability to demonstrate to the buyer why your property is worth what you are asking for it. Your property plan, your walkthrough, House doctoring, adding to your offer, and knowing your property like the back of your hand all go towards achieving this end. It allows you to tell him what's really on offer in terms of value, but there are two sides to this coin. Knowing all the reasons why you're selling allows you to know for yourself what's really on offer regarding the price he offers you. Once you're both very clear about these two aspects and how they come into play, a successful agreement and negotiation should be much easier.

The internet is full of tricks and tips as to how to come to an agreement in a negotiation. There's absolutely nothing to be lost from reading these articles. But what I will say is that for every trick and tip that tells you how to get one over on the buyer, there will be somebody like me on the other side giving the buyer tricks and tips on how to get one over on the seller.

The real answer to the question is actually much, much simpler. Come to an agreement where you're both happy. Neither of you should be dancing around the room like Leonardo Dicaprio's portrayal of Jordan Belfort in the movie 'The Wolf of Wall Street' laughing at how you got one over on the seller or the buyer. What you should both walk away with is the contentment and happiness that you definitely were not taken for a ride, robbed, tricked, or scammed and that you got a great value in the purchasing or sales process which worked for you based on a full understanding of your wants and your real reasons to buy or sell. That's the key to negotiation. You can both celebrate the sale, so whilst they are moving into the house and enjoying their house warming party, you will be checking your bank account, happy in the knowledge that you now have the ability to move on and do the things that you wanted to do which are more important to you that owning the property.

What can you afford to sell for?

What can you afford to sell for?

In exactly the same way that many buyers don't do their numbers correctly, a lot of sellers don't do their numbers correctly either.

Your sales price has to be a derivative of the following things;

How much you owe on your mortgage (in most, but not all cases, your mortgage will need to be completely paid when you sell your property). If you have an early redemption on your mortgage, you may have to actually pay back the full mortgage plus a penalty for not continuing to pay the mortgage to its full term.

You will need to add all of your selling costs together; being completely honest with yourself, this will include all of the costs of advertising and cosmetic refurbishment (House doctoring) you did in order to achieve the sale.

In Spain, it is the seller who pays the real estate agent, so you can add 5% to the amount that you want to receive in order to pay the real estate agents fees. If you are a good seller who is proactive and you follow some of the suggestions that we make here, you will also have other advertising costs such as Facebook Ad costs, other Online portal advertising costs, local media advertising costs, or the cost of other things that you used to try to sell your property; you will have your solicitors costs.

You have to include the cost of the valuation if you have your own valuation or home inspection done

In fact, any and all of the suggestions in this book and things that we have not suggested here but you tried, if they cost you money, they should be included in your calculation when you are deciding your sales price.

Then, of course, you have to factor in the government taxes. Oh no, no, no, no!!!! Don't you think for one second that the government is going to allow you to make a penny even out of your own property without taking a slice of the profit? So factor in how much of your profit the government is going to take once you have sold. Here in Spain, we have some pretty vicious taxes for property sales; we have both local Government and Central government taxes. Central government tax, which can add up to about 24% of the profits from the sale, and a Plusvalia tax, which is a local government tax that is based on the town councils appraisal of what the property is worth (not the actual sales price or profit, yes I know!!!), which until recently was being charged to people who lost money when they sold.

So these are the things that you have to take into consideration before you've set your sales price. If you are not going to be able to sell for a profit, you need to know this in advance, be resolved to the fact, and be absolutely clear and honest with yourself about it (this is why you need this information). Don't pretend that some of the costs aren't true or ignore other costs and pretend that they're not real or relevant. If you paid them, they are, and they represent the truth regarding if you are actually going to make anything when you sell.

Once you've worked out what the true costs of sale will be, you will know if you're going to actually make a profit out of the sale of your property, if you're going to just break even, or if you're going to make a loss.

It is at this point that you will need to go back to your, 'Why do you want to sell document.' This will help to make the relevance of this information clear. People want to sell the houses for different reasons and making a profit is only one and most often not the most important reason for most sellers. Knowing your personal 'why' is key to your ability to set a price that will allow you to fulfil it regardless of the external pressures such as ego-driven bragging rights or keeping up with the Jones. Because if you don't need to sell for a profit, if peace of mind, dissolving an estate, moving on from a failed relationship, or migrating to another area, for example, are your priorities, then you can sell for enough to cover your costs and take the loss in your personal finances as a cost of getting the things that you really wanted, which was to be free of the legal obligation of the property.

Alternatively, if you need a profit because the whole point of the sale was to do something else with the money, then you may decide that once all the sales costs have been seriously taken into consideration since there won't be a profit or enough of a profit to do what you had intended to do, you no longer want to sell at all. This will save not only you but also the estate agent and everybody else involved in the process the hassle and frustration of you pricing your property too high for the market so that you can sell it for the profit you need to go forward with your other venture. In most cases, this approach ends in the property being stuck and then eventually taken off the market with weeks, if not months, of agitation, annoyance, frustration, and stress caused to everyone in the process.

If you're in negative equity and it is clear that in addition to the loss of your personal deposit and buying and selling costs, that the realistic sales price of your property won't even create enough money to repay the mortgage loan which you owe to the bank or monies owed to other financial institutions from which your borrowed using the property as collateral, then you have two choices. You can again decide that you're not going to sell or at least not make a conventional sale, and then at this point, you can start to examine some of the creative strategies (such as the techniques and strategies that we specialise in), which will allow you to resolve your problems of ownership such as responsibility, stress and pressure and inability to meet payments, gaining the freedom from them and your property and getting your life back so that you can finally go forwards towards a future free from financial imprisonment and worry.

If your main focus, the number one thing you want to solve, is the hassle of owning the property, then you may, like many of the people we have helped, decide that our creative property sales strategies are for you. This can be done whether you have a mortgage or not, whether you are in positive or negative equity, regardless of if you have debts on the property and even if the property is in need of repairs.

Some people sell the property just to pay back the mortgage, even though they make no money out of it or have to put in funds from their own cash reserves to complete the sale.

Creative property sales strategies are also a perfect solution to this type of scenario because rather than paying money to get rid of the problem, we can help you get rid of the problem and possibly even pay you a small profit in situations where conventional real estate sales strategies could not.

One of the strategies we use is negotiating with the bank to 'write down the loan' (get the bank to agree to accept less money than the amount you actually owe in return for cancelling the loan), just to allow you to sell the property. This works for banks because it saves them from having to repossess the property, which is a very time-consuming and very costly process, and also allows them to have a client who may be struggling to make the payments or even behind on their payments off their books. Banks are very astute organisations, so having a business representing you will usually bring a better result than representing yourself, yet, either way, a clever bank will allow you to try to write off 10 to 15% of what you owe them in order to sell the property rather than having to repossess you with all the associated hassle, costs and time that it will require to do so, and if they do, we will have the buyer waiting to buy the property at this pre-discounted price which often allows them to pay you something to make it worth your while. This is just one of the ways in which our creative techniques and strategies help turn loss-making situations into profit for our customers, and it all starts with you, the seller knowing precisely what you can afford to sell for and why.

So this is the reason you must know the absolute true cost of selling your property. What you can really sell for, and then apply this to the main reason you want to sell and work out if selling your property is still the right thing to do. Once you have completed this procedure, if it is still right for you to sell, then price it accordingly, follow the rest of the advice in this book and get the job done. You will now have all of the information you need with regards to what you can do when it comes to pricing, putting together the plan, your limits when negotiating and your end goal, so just follow the direction in which these markers point, and you will get the result.

If not, then take it off the market and wait for better economic circumstances and if you are not in a position to do this, then get in touch and let us explore the creative strategies and solutions which may turn your losing situation into a winning one.

SELLING COSTS

Ok so in order to be able to know what we can afford to sell for, let's have a quick look at the selling process, what you need to do, what documents you will need to have and the costs that will be involved.

The costs of selling a property in Spain are the following;

Legal Fees

Most lawyers charge anywhere between 1% & 2% (+ IVA =VAT) of the price, Most lawyers will ask you for some money on account once you have signed their letter of engagement and completed any AML documents which they need you to sign. They will then take the balance of their fee on completion of the sale directly from the monies transferred for completion

Government Taxes

Spain like most of the countries in the Iberian peninsula is infamous for its complicated and seemingly inexplicable taxation system so the information presented here is for guidance purposes only and we strongly recommend that you seek the professional advice of an accountant, a tax adviser or

Gestore for up to date advice on the current Spanish legislation and regulation as it applies to Taxation

Local Government tax aka Plusvalia

This one off tax is paid to the local Ayuntamiento and has been the cause of much controversy over the last 12 years.

Based on the value of the land on which the property is sat it is an estimation of the increase in this value since the property was last sold? The calculation is based on a mixture of your period of ownership and the cadastral value aka the ground and the location of the property. This tax was the cause of much controversy in the years following the Great Recession of 2008 where some property values fell by up to 74% yet where given a Plus Valia based on their previous market price even though the current sales price was significantly less and the seller could demonstrate a financial loss from the sale. This has been the cause of new government guidelines which has in most areas seen this practice reduced to the level of almost being eradicated

NON-RESIDENTS: Capital Gains Tax

When a property is sold the buyer is obliged to retain 3% of the purchase price in order to ensure that the seller pays his tax (Yes I know), If the buyer fails in this obligation and you the seller does a midnight flit from the country then it is the buyer who will be held responsible for this cost and as such you will never see a property purchase overseen by a lawyer worth his salt would does not ensure that this 3% retention at sale is accounted for

Once retained this 3% of the sales price must be paid to the Spanish Tax Authorities as the first installment of the Seller´s Capital Gains Tax liability from the sale.

Unlike the fun and games played with the Plus Valia, If the seller can demonstrate a loss from the sale or that their capital gains bill should be less than this 3% then officially the difference can be reclaimed although I have yet to find anyone who had successfully achieved this, in fact due to the officiousness of the Spanish government system I don't even know anyone who has tried. If all you are liable for is 3% or even less, most sellers will just wipe their mouth, pay the 3%, take the rest of their profits and call it a good day.

If you made a profit on the sale of your property then as a non resident you will be taxed at the rate of 19% on the full amount of capital gains enjoyed (or based on your new tax bill not as enjoyed as was previously thought)

You have four months from the date of completion at Notary to make your capital gains declaration and either pay the full amount of 19% tax on your Net profit from the sale or seek a rebate on the 3% retained at Notary as part of completion

Here is where a good Lawyer and or Tax accountant will be worth their weight in gold. All costs incurred in the purchase of the property, the running and maintenance of the property and the final sale of the property are deductible expenses. These include purchase transfer tax, notary fees, Land registry fees, legal and real estate agent fees, refurbishment costs or any renovation and maintenance on the property for which you have original VAT invoices.

SPANSH TAX RESIDENTS Capital Gains Tax

Spanish tax residents are charged subject to the scale below:

€0-€6,000 – 19% of the net Capital gains from the sale

€6,000-€50,000 - 21% of the net Capital gains from the sale

€50,000 onwards 23% of the net Capital gains from the sale

Again all costs which occurred from the purchase, sale, maintenance and renovation of the property are deductible expenses subject to the provision of Vat invoices.

ADDITIONAL RULES: The main home exemption

Like many other European countries Spanish tax residents are exempt from paying capital gains tax on the sale of their property only in the circumstances where they sell their main residence and use the money to buy another main residence. To be eligible for this tax relief you must have lived in the property you are selling for at least 3 years and use the money to buy another property which you use as your main home within 2 years of completion of the initial sale at Public Notary. Good news for EU members is that your new residence does not have to be in Spain for you to qualify for this tax relief. As long as it is in an the European Economic Area (EEA) country you will qualify so not great news for UK sellers post Brexit then but Hey Ho such is life.

Over 65 Spanish resident exemptions:

A tax resident in Spain over the age of 65 has certain advantages for Capital Gains Tax purposes. If you are over the age of 65 and you sell a property that has been your main residence you will not pay capital gains tax. This applies as long as the property sold had been your main residence for more than 3 years and still applies even if you do not re-invest the proceeds in another property.

Mortgage cancellations fees

Most Banks have early redemption fees for mortgages so if you are selling a property with a number of years on the mortgage make sure you contact the bank and confirm the penalty which you will have to pay. Newer banking regulations have gone some way to standardizing these fees making the usually amount 0.5% of the loan but variations do still exist so be sure to check it out

Real Estate Agency Fee

Depending on their position in the market, level of prestige and level of marketing a Real estate agent will either charge you a fee to list and market your property or may be willing to list your property for free.

All agents will charge the balance of their fees upon completion which again may vary with the most common sales fees being between 5% and 7% Plus IVA

So these are the costs and taxes associated with selling a property from a legal standpoint, but from a personal standpoint you really should include everything that you have spent on the property since you bought it, yes the whole kit and Caboodle. All of the running costs such as IBI, Basura, Community fees, all maintenance costs such as repaints and boiler replacement, and all upgrades such as refurbishments.

Strictly speaking this list is for property investors as every cost associated with an investment property should be taken away from the sales price in order to see the true level of profit made by the investment over the period of ownership. If you lived in the property or only had it for personal use then you should definitely take some of these costs into consideration as things bought for personal use and so not applicable as costs associated with the sale but I find that the best way to do this is to list absolutely everything that the property has cost you and then once you have an exhaustive list decide what you think is really applicable and cross off what you think is not.

Top Tips for taking the responsibility in selling your Property

- Acknowledge that selling your property is your responsibility

- Write down a list of at least 10 reasons why you want to sell

- Write down a list of at least 10 real reasons behind the reasons you want to sell

- Do an honest calculation of what you can afford to sell for including all selling costs

CHAPTER 2: MAKE A HOME SELLING PLAN

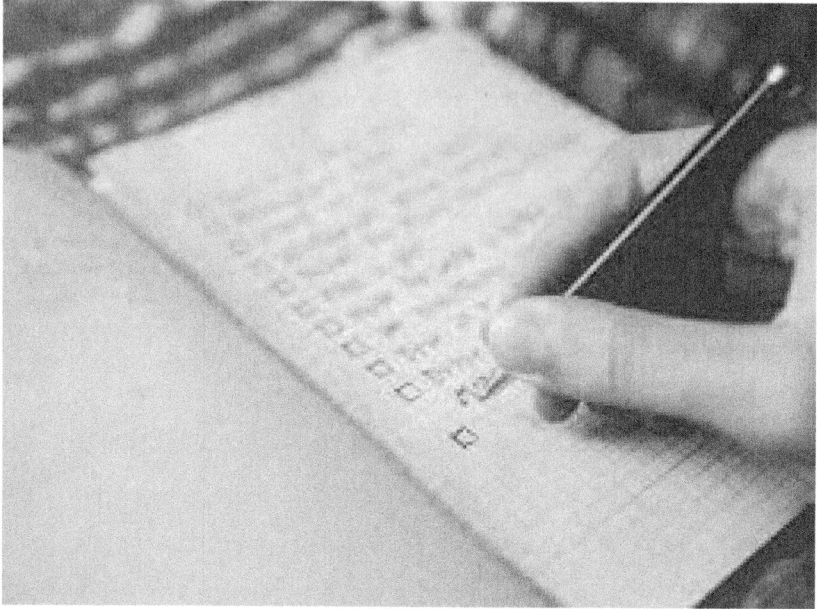

If you fail to plan, you plan to fail. Have you ever heard this before? Yes, then why do so many people put their property on the market for sale with no plan at all other than to give it to an estate agent and cross their fingers that it sells on time and on price?

As you will discover in this book, if you want to sell your property (in normal times but especially if you want to sell in a recession), you are going to have to take responsibility; therefore, you are going to have to do some of the work.

This work starts with making a written plan of how you are going to sell your home.

Make a plan of your home as if you were a new developer selling it. If you have never paid any attention to the techniques of new build development sales, now is the time to start. They have Brochures and floor plans, information about the surrounding area, and bullet-point lists of the features of their properties. But more importantly than what they have to show outwardly, they have a similar plan internally with all of this information which is what they use to inform their marketing department on how and where to market the property and their sales team to on whom and what to focus on when trying to sell it

This is the type of document that you need to have

Your Home selling plan doesn't have to be a long document; in fact, it shouldn't be. Make it as short as possible. The point is not to create a literary work of art; the point is to help you because, in order to sell a property, you need to know what you're selling.

Now you may think, 'I know what I'm selling doofus; I'm selling my family home.'

Yes, I know that. But the buyer doesn't.

The buyer, having done their research, will have seen hundreds of homes already. Homes on property portals, homes on real estate agent websites, homes in magazines, homes that follow them around the internet via retargeted digital marketing ads, homes on viewings, and they're all been presented in exactly the same way.

So just selling your home might be correct from your personal perspective, but in terms of the market, you are not. In terms of the market, your one-use family home may be a 4-bedroom house perfect for summer investment rentals or a city-based 4-

bed student accommodation opportunity. The one-bed starter apartment bought in an inner-city that you didn't really want but was all that you and your wife could afford at the time might be a perfect Bachelor pad for the up-and-coming young city executive. Your 2-bed summer rental investment based out of town and previously marketed to nature-loving holidaymakers might be the perfect retirement apartment for empty nesters who have decided to retire overseas.

Looking at the property that you are selling objectively opens up new opportunities for getting it sold, and a home selling plan is the starting point that will allow you to see your property not as it has always been used but as potential buyers might see it. This is what the internal part of the home selling plan does for you.

And what will it do for the buyer? Well, you may be selling your bachelor pad to upgrade and move in with your girlfriend, but the potential buyer doesn't know that. Your potential buyer sees hundreds of homes every day, most of which have all been presented exactly the same way. You need to create something different that stands out, and the way you do that is by knowing what you're selling and who it most appeals to.

How do you know what you're selling? Well, you need to approach it from the viewpoint of a salesperson. Anybody familiar with the film 'The Wolf of Wall Street' will be familiar with the line, 'Sell me this pen.'

Salesmen have many different variations of what to focus on in order to achieve this.

What is different about the pen?

What is unique about the pen?

Usually, the best answer is, what is the value of the pen to the person you're selling it to?

What can the pen do for them?

What are its benefits?

Additionally, compared to all the other pns available, why is this pen better than the others, and how is it better than the one you are currently using?

Now that you've proven that the pen has all the benefits that the buyer needs and is unique and better than its competition, how will you help them in their purchase of the pen so that it can be purchased easily and they can get all of the benefits and improvements it brings into their lives.

This type of plan is what we do with our direct selling clients. We sell their homes by extracting the essential information from them sufficient to build out a home selling plan which is a sales plan for their home. We then use that plan as the basis for our marketing campaign to get interests in their property and then use the marketing and the aspects uncovered from the home selling plan to direct the sales. This has proven highly effective. I mean, no sales plan is guaranteed, but if you haven't done one already, you should instinctively see how much more powerful an actual plan to sell your home is than what you've probably done up until now, which is to give it to a lot of real estate agents and hope that they have a plan.

In my experience, having spent more time selling than studying sales, most Real estate agents just look at the features of your property and go out into the market to sell it armed with that. As the owner of multiple businesses and a business consultant, trainer, and mentor, I have studied sales for over two decades. I would suggest that putting more into the sales process is the only way to guarantee getting more out of it.

In his seminal book on selling, *Soft Selling in a hard world*, Gerry Vas tells salesmen to never, ever just sell the features of a product; you must sell its benefits. When you list your house with a real estate agent, you're hoping that he knows this, but you've got no idea if he does. Most salesmen are distinctly average; hence, they have distinctly average businesses and distinctly average lives (many try to hide this with expensive watches, cars, and clothes which they really can't afford), as opposed to the best salesmen whose businesses and lives are anything but average. The reason it (being distinctly average) works out for them is that yours is not the only house which they have to sell. They have several houses on their books to sell, and amongst this list, they have a number of stuck houses that they cannot sell, but they keep on their books because it costs them nothing to do so, and who knows, they might get lucky and find a buyer for it one day. So in order for them to keep being in business, they only have to sell a proportion of the properties on their books on a monthly basis, maybe two or three from the 20 or 30 they have listed. If you add the Multiple Listing Systems, which exists in Spain and most countries to this equation, you will realise that these guys don't even have to sell any of the twenty properties they have listed personally. They have access to thousands of other real estate agents who can find the buyer for them and still make half of the sales commission. I will discuss the multiple listing system in greater detail later in the book, but for now, all you need to know is that for the agents registered on the system, they have the majority of the properties (if not every single property listed for sale) available between them including properties from New build developers and companies. So, if they are anything like me, they don't even have to specialise in the region where their office is based or where they live and have expertise. I always sold properties from Malaga right through to La Linea on the border of Gibraltar, which gave me the maximum opportunity to make money from a sale anywhere along the Costa del Sol, but that's not all. I have also sold properties in Murcia, Alicante, Barcelona, Madrid, and other Iberian countries such as Portugal, Cyprus, Greece, and Italy, all using the leverage provided by the various MLS systems.

The point I am making is that with such a resource at the real estate agent's fingertips, a resource which allows them to use other agent's properties and buyers to make money from their listings or vice versa, selling your home, in particular, is not of great importance to them. But selling your home is of great importance to you, so you really need to have your own sales plan for your home.

So what should your Home selling plan include?

Like all business documents, this will vary. As a business mentor, I can assure you that no two business plans are alike. They vary with the writer's skills, focus, and personality, but there are some essential aspects a good one needs to have, and a good Home selling plan is the same. Every good home sales plan needs a few essential items, so what I can do is provide you with the outline and the blueprint of what your home selling plan needs to include.

The sales plan for your home needs to have the following sections;

Property type

The details of the property as a real estate agent would state them. The number of bedrooms and bathrooms it has etc. Also, the type of property, is it an apartment or villa and the date it was constructed, is it from a particular building era?

Price

State the price early, so if your internal document is adapted to an actual sales brochure as part of your own promotion, you can save yourself and the buyer a lot of time. My pet hate is the fact that almost all estate agents promote their properties by listing the property type, features with glittery sales, putting the price at the end as if any of the preceding information is going to change the fact that you can't actually afford it. Don't do this. Tell them the price at the outset, and if it's within their budget and they can actually buy it, then proceed to convince them of why.

Location

Another thing that so many agents get wrong is that they leave the location until last rather than using it as a way to filter out prospective buyers before they get too far into the process. Now I do accept that on occasion, a buyer has been known to change the location that they are buying in based on price considerations, but these are not your best clients. Your best potential buyers are the ones who have already done their area research and decided that the location of your property is where they want to buy. The habit of concealing locations or at least exact locations is not the privacy issue you might assume it to be. It actually goes back to the bad old days of real estate when if you put the full address of a property in an advert or even the street, a rival real estate agent (or sometimes even a buyer) would track the property down and approach the seller to offer her a better deal and steal it from you. I say the bad old days, but in fact, this still happens now, so even I usually only give an area location, not a full address, but whatever you use, make sure that the information is useful to the buyer, and as you are selling your own property and no one can steal the listing from you or make a direct offer to you based on cutting you out, you can be as precise as your personal comfortability, and privacy level allows.

The surrounding area

This includes transport links, distance to town, parks, areas of natural beauty, and all essential features of the property, and we will deal with this much more in the later chapters.

Validation of the price

Why is it worth what you are asking for it? If it is worth that much, you had better be prepared to prove it. If it is not, and you are just trying it on, then this is the time to get real. Proof or the legitimacy of your asking price should include comparable properties which are similar properties to the one you are selling, which have recently sold for the same price, or preferably even more. If no comparisons of properties recently sold are available, then use examples of similar properties offered for sale.

A floor plan

This is not essential but very useful not just for the potential buyer but also for your internal sales plan as it will help you plan your walkthrough and method of touring the property when you begin to get direct prospects. If you don't have an original, can you get one made or even make a non-professional (not to scale) one yourself? Your floor plan can be created in one of the online drawing tools available or a PC package, and although it may not look professional, it will still be better than the properties which have none at all.

The features of your home

This should include all of the best aspects of your property for sale. The fact that it has three rooms in the urbanisation of mainly two beds, the roof terrace with the panoramic views, the sea view from the living room, the utility room, the fact that you extended the conservatory, the spacious garden, the walking distance to the shops, the nearby school, the walking distance to the beach. All of these things are features of your particular property, and the creation of your home selling report is an excellent way of forcing yourself to see all of the great aspects of your home. You should aim for at least 20 features and within the 20 at least 5 Key ones which make your property better than other near-identical properties on the same urbanisation.

The benefits that these features provide

Here is a quick tip that most salespeople do not know. You find the benefits of what you are selling by simply taking the features and explaining their advantages to the buyer. This is done very easily by writing sentences about your property where you call out the feature and then explain the benefit that this feature will bring to the potential buyer. Taking a few examples from our list of features above, this is what it should look like;

Your property has three rooms in the urbanisation of mainly two beds which not only gives you more space for the same price but means that you can earn more in rentals than if you bought the two beds because three beds allow you to rent not only to small families but extended families on holiday and golfing groups as well.

Or talking about the distance to the beach, you could say; 'walking distance to the beach gives this property the greater potential of full occupancy when rented because properties closer to the beach rent more quickly, they rent at a premium but being close to the beach is also great for self-use buyers with elderly parents or children who will be able to go to the beach without the fear of being too tired to return safely or without difficulty.'

So as you will see, extracting your property's benefits is a simple case of listing the features and then asking a simple if not obstinate question, 'so what?'

If you ask 'so what?' or perhaps a more polite 'and how does that benefit me?' to every feature on your list, you will soon find yourself with an amazing list of benefits which can be used to ethically persuade your potential buyer that your property is the one for them.

Know your surroundings

Just like doing a walkthrough of your home, you must also know your surroundings. This comes back to the power of location, location, location; so good they named it thrice.

Yes, most real estate agents will tell you that your geographic location is the most crucial factor in selling your home, so yes, you need to know all of the pros and cons about the area in which your property resides; I mean, who else should, you're the one who lives there so you're the one who should know it.

Ok, so I know that it's also very possible that you are selling an investment home and maybe you don't know everything about the area, or maybe, since you bought it and the surroundings have changed. Well, tough, get to know, find out, ask around, learn it by hook or by crook, or risk missing out on the biggest-selling tool you will have to get your house reserved and sold.

Make sure you know the surroundings of your home, not just to counteract any negativity but also to promote positivity. Be able to promote that the nearby school (the one that creates noise at recess and makes the road busy at times when it's the 'school run') is also one of the best schools in the area, making your property perfect for young parents migrating to the country with primary school-aged children. If this is the case, then your potential buyers need to know about it, and you can't just rely on your estate agent to know; you need to know about it too.

Similarly, know that restaurant at the end of the road that won the second-best Tapas awards on the coast. If it has been featured in any press, have this available to prove the point.

You need to know that your local beach is a blue flag beach and has Soccoristas (lifeguards) making sure that everyone using it is safe between the months of June and October, which is great because most local beaches only provide lifeguards until the end of September, but because your area has a micro-climate, it stays warmer for longer which attracts more elderly tourists in search of Winter sun, so the Ayuntamiento extended the lifeguard season. Ok, I just made this up, but if this were true of your area, local climate, tourist demographic, and local government policy, then you would need to know all of this too.

You need to know all of the things in your area that make it very safe or safer when compared to the other areas where they may consider buying. You need to know the things about your area that are not very safe and what can be done to mitigate the risks, not just for you but also for other types of families and demographics, such as parents with young children or senior citizens. If it's unsafe, what is it? What have people done about it? Is there a community watch programme that helps keep your home safe? If there is, how do they join it? You need to know all of this. You need to know everything that you can about the surrounding areas of the home you have for sale, particularly in terms of the things that would attract your kind of buyer.

So again, once you've done your research and know the kind of person who is most likely to buy your home (this is called your Avatar, and we will focus on this in greater depth in the marketing section of this book), you need to know the kinds of things that will attract them.

If you are having difficulty defining this perfect, most likely buyer of your home, you can do it the other way around. You can collate all of the information for your whole marketing plan and then look specifically at the information regarding the surroundings of your home (location, location, location), and use this information to work out what kind of people or persons would be attracted by these specific attributes and benefits.

Then once you've worked out who would be attracted by a home in your area with its particular features, specifications, location, and surroundings, you will be able to make an informed guess as to your target market in terms of what kinds of people will be most likely to want to buy the property you have to sell. You can then make any of the adjustments or changes you need to do internally or externally to increase the curb appeal and walkthrough appeal to these specific buyers, as well as having all the information and answers to the questions that people from that market will require when choosing a home, out of a shortlist of comparables.

You can also arrange to have your marketing person or arrange the marketing that you are doing yourself to target towards this specific buying demographic since it is the one which has been identified as the most likely to buy.

A critique of your house

This is the hardest part of the process. We know it's your home, and it's lovely, but other people are going to want to do stuff with your house and are going to look at it a tad more objectively. Being critical of the property you have for sale is a way of pointing out all the wrong things with it, or at least not as attractive as its competitors. If you are going to sell it, you really need to know this list because even if you put your head in the sand and pretend that these faults and weaknesses do not exist, your potential buyer is sure to see them and bring them up, and the bringing up of all of the things wrong with your product in sales is called objections.

As a salesman, we learn to overcome objections before they happen, i.e., we are aware of the drawbacks, expect the prospective buyer to point the drawback or problem out, and as such, we have already prepared the answer to overcome or resolve the issue even before it is mentioned.

So if you know in your heart that your bathroom is a little bit small and cramped to use, having identified this when you looked at your properties features or did the floor plan, being honest about the problem when you do the critique of your property and thus having an answer prepared for this criticism, you had neutralised the problem before it occurred.

'As you will see, this bathroom is a little bit small, but it is the 3rd bathroom in the property, whereas most of the others on this urbanisation have only two. So it's not big enough to dance in, but it has been invaluable when we have had family over or friends over for drinks. Plus, if you look at the floor plans, you will see that it backs onto the garden, so there is room to extend it if you wanted to.'

This is an example of overcoming an objection before it even occurred. The objection which would have stopped the buyer from buying your home is the small bathroom, but you explained it away in terms of a feature (that it is actually an additional bathroom, so they are getting one more, not one less), and then followed up with the benefit that this feature has given you and will give to them. Then you also provided a method of resolving the obstacle in the long term if they so wished.

Now I appreciate that the above example might not be true of every property, so your overcome might be more along the lines of to simply say that you are aware of the fact that the 2nd bathroom is a little bit small, but most of this is down to inefficient design, and you have spoken to a builder who says that it can be improved to provide more space for… (Give the budget), which you are willing to remove off the sales price if they are really interested in buying.

There you go, objection solved before the potential buyers even made it. They now trust you more. They believe that you are genuine. You're not just another greedy house seller out to make a buck. You are somebody who genuinely knows the pros and cons of their property and is willing to be fair with regards to a buyer in alleviating them.

The ability to do all of this comes from the production of your home selling plan. The ability to overcome objections and negative comments which come from your prospective buyers is very powerful because it not only builds their confidence in you, but it removes the reasons they cannot or don't want to buy, and if you can remove all of the reasons to say no, the only thing left to say is yes.

Some people say that 'a sale is an exchange of enthusiasm.' That is true, so your sales plan should be enthusiastic. If you don't love your property already, learn to love it and put that into the sales plan. But the sales plan should also be an exchange of trust. Once they've seen the effort that you put into the sales plan, they will have more trust in you.

One last thing about the sales plan, I mentioned before, and I will repeat. It does not have to be a document that you present to the buyer. It can just be a document that you create for yourself to help you plan and execute the sale of your property. But once you have put all of the efforts into making this personal sales document, you might as well adapt it for potential buyers, as this represents a wonderful example of leverage.

Yes, it will take you some time to do it (unless you hire someone else to do it for you), but it will only need to be done once. Think of all the houses that have been on the market for nine months. Think of all the viewings and all the phone calls or contacts they've had. And every single time somebody calls, the seller has to go through the same process of talking about the pros and cons, the good, the bad, and the features and benefits of the house.

Once complete, you will have a house selling plan that you can send out to people to do all of that for you, freeing up your time to do some of the other exercises in this book. And more importantly, only when people have seen your Home sales plan or sales brochure and are genuinely interested in buying it will they come and book a viewing.

This allows you to save time by using it to prequalify the people who view your home, so you're not only saving time on wasted viewings, you're getting better quality potential buyers coming to visit, which is bringing you closer to a sale every time you open your front door

Top Tips for Making a Home Selling Plan

- Make the plan written

- Include all aspects of your property internally (Number of bedrooms, garden etc)

- Include all aspects of your property externally (Location, distance from amenities etc)

- Include or make a floor plan

- Use your plan to critique your property thoroughly

CHAPTER 3: YOUR PROPERTY SELLING POWER TEAM

Before we dig into the nuts and bolts of getting your house sold, I just want to take a few chapters to describe your property selling power team. This is the team of professionals which I advise you to secure and use in order for your property sale to go forward as quickly and profitably as possible. Depending on your price point, preference and circumstances, you may choose to employ the services of all of these professionals or maybe just a few, but I wanted to highlight all of the ones that I think you should use in a best of all worlds scenario. I will make a point of stating very clearly which of these services are optional and which are essential and thus non-negotiable.

Get a Lawyer

If you're selling a house, unless you have a Spanish Law degree, get a lawyer.

It is not a strict legal requirement to use a lawyer if you are buying or selling a property, and I admit that if I had to choose, I would say that the buyer needs a lawyer more than the seller.

But that said, I still recommend that you get a lawyer to represent you in the sale.

Your property may well be one of the biggest, most expensive assets you sell, and to gamble the safety of this sale and the income from it on the 2% in legal fees you will save by not engaging legal assistance to make sure that the process is swift and legally compliant, it is a false and dangerous economy.

If you don't know what you're doing, you could be leaving yourself open to being completely screwed over, and if that happens as a result of your lack of knowledge or inability to understand what has been agreed or the process, it will be nobody's fault but your own.

So if we are agreed that you need to use a lawyer, you will obviously need to use your own lawyer, duh!!!

Well, actually, this is not always true. In Spain, it is perfectly legal for one lawyer to represent both parties, so technically, the buyer can use your lawyer, or you could use the buyers'. This scenario works best in cases such as new developments where the developer may hire a top-flight law firm to oversee all of the sales in the complex. This law firm will be big and prestigious and have all of the information regarding the site, the planning permission, the licenses, and the sales particulars in one place, so it is a good economy for buyers to use them as well (if they are trustworthy which is not always the case, due diligence still applies), as they can often provide services to the buyer at a lower price because they have all of the information already so do not need to do the research again for each buyer.

Like all things, there are times when this system works well and other times where it is less advisable, but what is a deal-breaker is that you, the seller use a lawyer for your property sale, which is non-negotiable.

Some estate agents will have their own reservation contracts. This is not a bad idea because they will want to get an interested party to reserve the property as soon as possible to make sure that the sale is locked in. Plus, reservation contracts are not really particularly complicated documents; they are really there to prove that you have an agreement to buy at a particular price. They serve to secure the property at an agreed price for the buyer, a price at which they can buy the property as long as their lawyer does not find anything illegal or untoward about it, and also to protect you, the seller, because if their lawyer does not find anything untoward about the property, but they decide not to continue with the purchase, you get to keep the reservation fee in lieu of the opportunity cost of having taken the property off the market for them when you might have been able to sell it to someone else.

It is the exchange at the private contracts stage where the buyer will pay the 10% deposit (which is your real security and a better representation of your opportunity costs) that you really need your own lawyer for, and since you are going to engage a legal representative anyway, you may as well have him in place right at the start when you put your property on the market. At this stage, the buyer's solicitor will need a list of the 'particulars that come with the sale,' legally binding information about the property, its freedom from debts, that the property is legal, built in an area zoned for residential property or that kind of construction, approved by planning and has a license of 1st occupation, that the property is definitely yours and you have the full rights to sell it among many other things.

This is why you absolutely need a lawyer to take care of this for you. Because as I pointed out before, your buyer will have a lawyer making sure that his interests are represented correctly, and an aggressive buyer's lawyer can manipulate the situation to the advantage of the buyer if you don't have an equally qualified person on your side of things to represent your interests.

Do not, and I repeat, do not use your real estate agent for this. No matter how fluent in Spanish they are (even if it's their natural tongue). Do not use a Gestore for this, no matter the fact that they are effectively bookkeepers or accountants and know a lot about property. And definitely do not use your mate Jerry down the pub because he sold his property last year and didn't use a lawyer, so he can help you out for the price of a Cerveza and a packet of pork scratching. You need a lawyer who is a member of the Law Society at the very least for the fact that if they make mistakes and something goes wrong, they will have their legal indemnity, which will allow them to pay you compensation in lieu of any loss of earnings you suffer from their mistakes.

Additionally, as every contract is different, you will need your lawyer to look at any documentation presented to them, and more importantly, your lawyer will draw up and present the contract for the private exchange for the buyer and his lawyer to look over.

I was going to include an example of a reservation contract and a private exchange contract in the notes, but then I realised that this would go against the core premise of this chapter, so I decided against it. Firstly, because these documents are not dictated by the government, the individual version used by your lawyer or their lawyer will vary depending on common practice, company culture, the region of Spain you are selling in, precedent, and the specific terms and requirements of your sale. It is this last part where the greatest danger lies. Contracts are negotiable, and having written a fair few myself; I have learned the hard way that the word 'and' inserted where you really meant 'or' can dramatically affect the outcome. When it comes to contracts, you need to be specific, and you need them correct, or as the old saying goes, you need all of your 'i's' dotted and your 't's' crossed.

There are a lot of things that you can do in terms of selling your property without the use of an estate agent, aka FSBO, and even though I do no advocate restricting yourself to FSBO, I definitely advocate doing all of them to help you to get your property sold. But what I definitely do not advocate for is potentially throwing all of this good work away right at the finish line by attempting to do something that you have not trained for (legal work) whilst competing with someone who has trained a minimum of seven years to do it. Imagine it was a game of tennis. You step onto the court, having never played the game. You just read few books and, of course, watched a few YouTube videos called 'How to be a millionaire tennis player and beat Rafa Nadal, Federer, and Djokovic in just six weeks, even if you have never played a single game of Tennis in your life.' Your opponent steps onto the court, not Rafa, or Roger, not even Tim (Henman post-Hip Operation). In fact, you've never heard of him, just an everyday guy with one exception. He is, in fact, a Tennis pro who trained for seven years at the Academy of Sports, has a pro license, and now works as a professional Tennis player training and competing every day.

You make the first serve, and the scores roll in. 40: Love, 40: Love, 40: Love, 40: Love, 40: Love. Set to pro guy. I think you can see where this is going (for all of you non-tennis aficionados, you'll lose badly without scoring a point).

And this is just the first game, but trust me, as sure as night follows day, even if you finally get a few points in, Game, Set, and Match will eventually go in his favour.

Do not scrimp on the important things and lose all of your hard work at the final hurdle (perhaps I should have used an Athletics analogy, oh well). Get yourself a lawyer, so when you finally do find that buyer willing to buy at a price and with the terms that you want, you get the agreement and process to be as watertight and seamless as possible and get your Spanish Property sold.

Get a mortgage broker.

This might seem absolutely counterintuitive, but as a strategy, it is just super powerful.

Your buyer may already have a mortgage broker, but then again, she might not, so it wouldn't hurt you to have someone in place that you can recommend to help them.

Again, you don't want to waste anybody's time but engaging a broker won't take a huge amount of his time.

For the broker, what you are doing is offering to bring business to them, i.e., if you find a buyer who needs a mortgage and does not already have a broker, you will recommend them. This has got to be worth the small amount of his time to look at the valuation on your property and give you an idea of what kind of mortgage he could get for your prospective buyer.

If you are going to go down this route, then the best plan would be to contact a mortgage broker, tell him your plan, tell him that you are going to market your home for sale yourself (as well as using an agent), and then use him to help you to find the Valuation company which he knows is already on the panel of the bank that he would use to get your buyer the mortgage and preferably recommend to you the particular valuation company who are giving the highest valuations on properties like yours or in your area. This will help you massively as finding the valuer yourself brings with it a much higher risk as there is no reason you will know which valuers are valuing high and which are infamous for giving low or undervaluations. But a good mortgage broker knows this exact information; his job depends on it. So armed with his advice, rather than risking your money, you are making an informed, calculated risk when getting your valuation done as it will be performed by the company most likely to value your property for more, hence, helping you to get the highest price from your buyer.

Some mortgage brokers will refuse your offer as they will not have the foresight to see the bigger picture. You're doing the buyers work for them, and like all businesses, especially IFA's and Broker know, referrals are cheaper than marketing, and every satisfied customer can be worth up to 5 referrals, meaning that if you recommend them to the buyer, they can expect another 2 to 5 clients as a result of your generosity. As you will not be asking for a marketing fee in terms of their business, this is free money, so if they are short-sighted and unaware of this fact, feel free to quote this chapter and remind them.

If you already have had your valuation done, then simply send your valuation to a mortgage broker and ask him if he works with banks that use this valuer. Ask him, based on the valuation, which of his lenders he thinks would be able to get your buyer a mortgage on your house.

Make no mistake, your eventual buyer may buy with cash or already have a bank or mortgage broker in place but having a valuation and your own preferred mortgage broker ready to assist could be the difference between being able to buy or not for some of the interested parties.

Having your own mortgage broker to recommend who knows everything about your property and already has a lender lined up is not an essential aspect of your power team, but if you choose to do it, you will soon see that it provides you with yet another safety net to make sure that you have contingency plans and options which allow you to catch all potential buyers and make the ability for them to buy your property as frictionless as possible.

Get a valuation

If your house has been stuck in a market and you are really frustrated with the low offers that you are getting, it might be worth proving what your house is worth by having your own valuation done.

Now, I know that you will have an opinion of what your home is worth, and the Estate agent will have given you an opinion of what the property is worth but let's keep it real for a minute. You are the seller, so your opinion is probably biased, and the real estate agent's opinion is often quite frankly bullshit. In fact, far too many of them give you a high predicted value for your house just to get the listing. They tell you what you want to hear just to get your house on their books, and then they market your house at that price (a price which they know that no one is going to pay). After a few months, when you ask what is going on? Why have you had so few viewings? And why haven't you had any offers? They will turn around and say, 'Well, the price is a bit high; we're selling houses for less in your area.' This is how they slowly whittle you down to the price they would have told you right at the outset if they didn't already know that in your refusal to accept reality, you wouldn't have got frustrated, refused to accept it and given the business to another liar instead of them.

It's a game that real estate agents have been playing since the first cave dwellings and when mud huts and straw houses were built. I've seen everybody fall for this from my own Father (even though I was already in real estate and told him exactly what they were doing), right through to so-called millionaire investors who still fall for this trick. For real estate listers, it is the gift that just keeps giving, and it works regardless of territory. I have seen people fall for the same thing in all of the areas in which I have worked; Portugal, Cyprus, England, and of course, Spain. If the term 'Boil a frog slowly' was not invented in real estate, it really should have been.

I must hasten to add that not all real estate agents do this. I recently offered a property to a handful of local real estate agents, and half of them refused to accept the property onto their books unless I accepted their rather modest valuation of what it should be marketed at. This was very refreshing and a great reminder that genuine, honest, and professional real estate agents are alive and well; they are just not spoken about a lot in my books. I do not focus on the good real estate agents because I don't need to protect you from them; I need to protect you from the tricks and scams of the ones who are not trustworthy and for these less trustworthy real estate agents promising to sell your property for more than its' worth is listing 101.

So how do you actually get a provable value of your home that you can use to negotiate with the buyer?

Well, the reality is that you have to follow the same process that the buyer will do. The buyer is no doubt going to make his own assessment of the value of your house using comparables that he has seen online and in the papers; more astute buyers may have checked the land registry to see the previous sales prices, but at the end of the day and luckily for you, the buyers' assessment of the value of your property is cemented in about as much quicksand as yours. Neither of you can really prove the validity of your opinion as you are both biased with self-interest.

But the true assessment that no one will argue with (even though it isn't always right) is the bank's assessment because if the bank is going to give a loan on the house, they have to value it and value it as correctly as possible. Therefore, the bank's assessment of the value of the property is usually taken as, if not the holy grail of its true valuation, at the very least, a decent valuation that can be relied upon.

Put simply, the bank is not going to do a valuation on a property and make a loan based on that valuation that loses them money, and with 60% or more loan to value, the bank has the most to lose. So as the valuation is the core component used to secure their money, and with so much at stake, the bank isn't going to do an incorrect valuation on a property if it can at all help it.

Therefore, at least from the bank's viewpoint, this valuation is going to be correct. They're not going to do a valuation that allows them to make a loan that's too high because in times of recessions, overvalued properties that they repossess will have to be sold for less than they lent to buy them, and they will lose money. Ok, ok, some of you may remember that this is exactly what they did in the early 2000s, which led directly to the Great Recession of 2008, but my point is that it has been stated by everybody from government officials to economists worldwide that they shouldn't have. And the results of doing so; people have lost their jobs, some have gone to jail, laws have been brought in to at least try to make it legally impossible to repeat, and everybody has promised never to do it again (well, at least that's what they say). So as overvaluation of property was at the heart of this recession, it demonstrates why in terms of security, at least, it's in their interest not to overvalue.

Similarly, although they may err on the side of caution, too low a valuation will either lose them business as the more money they lend, the more they make in interest payments over the term of the loan (often a staggering three times the initial loan amount), a substantial amount of money of which they greedily want every penny. Or even worse, a low valuation could make the purchase unfeasible as the buyer will not have enough deposit to buy at all, and if the valuation is really, really low, a well-off buyer may decide that they no longer need the mortgage and just buy it with cash. In this way, overall, it is in their interest to do a correct valuation.

So since the buyer who is buying with a mortgage is more likely than not going to value your property based on a bank valuation, as the seller, why don't you just get one done and then use it as the basis for the sales price you market your property at?

The important thing to know here is that banks do not actually value the properties. They use independent professional valuation companies to do the valuation for them. Each bank uses a number of these independent valuation companies, which they trust and therefore use, and this is called their panel of valuers. Now, as a seller, you can't get a bank valuation on your property unless you're going for a remortgage, but if you are not really looking for one, then I wouldn't advise that you waste a bank's time like that. What you can do is contact a mortgage broker (hence the reason he has been put in your power team) or the bank directly to find out which valuation companies are on that bank's panel of values. You can then contact the valuation company directly and pay them to do a valuation of your property. Paying the valuation company directly will cost you more than it will cost the potential buyer if he requests the valuation through the bank, but this few hundred euros more in valuation costs could make you thousands more in profit from a higher sales price.

What will having your own professional valuation do?

Having your own professional valuation of your property will give you a bank accredited (at least from the terms of being done by the exact same valuer that a bank would have sent out if a buyer had asked for a loan to buy your property) valuation.

This now gives you an impartial benchmark as to what your property is worth. So now, when your buyer comes in with a cheeky low offer (and he will) of 30 to 35% below your asking price (even though the current market value is already depressed 20% below the long term market value making the offer 50% below what you paid for it), you can present him with a recent valuation and say;

'Look, two months ago, this property was valued at 20% more than that, and that's a conservative bank valuation. That is the reason I won't accept your offer, but if you want to get a loan to buy this property, what you can do is take a copy of this valuation to… (give him the name of the bank that uses the valuation company on their panel), and use it to get the maximum bank loan.'

As I said before, in terms of impartiality, the bank valuation is seen as the pinnacle, so you will now have set the benchmark price around in which real negotiations can begin. No more 'fannying' around with ridiculous low ball offers for you, the seller, and equally no more suffering way higher than current market valuation expectations of price from you, the seller. The bank valuation, or at least the valuation by the valuation company used by banks in your area, is the great equalizer.

In this way, getting your own valuation done becomes a powerful negotiation tool that can work very well, particularly if the buyer is using a bank to finance the purchase of property, and it can also definitely work very well in conjunction with some of the other tools and tricks and tips that we present in this book so although not an essential, based on its power in negotiations a great thing to have if you can afford it.

Know the selling process.

This might sound silly, but it's absolutely true. Your buyer will probably not know the sales process, so he will have to believe what is told to him by his estate agent or lawyer.

Nevertheless, if it is his first purchase in Spain, he will feel a certain amount of anxiety at getting the correct information, so you can be a great comfort to the buyer

Think about it, if the information about the buying process that you are telling the buyer is congruent with the process that he is being told by his estate agent and lawyer, then you will add to his feelings of safety and security

Even better, if your competitor tells a different story or they're demanding different things, especially things that he is less likely to be happy about, which of these two houses is he going to buy?

So know the sales process. Know the things that he should have been told by his real estate agent and lawyer and confirm that they are true. You may think that knowing the buying process is not your business, but it is; you are going to benefit from it after all.

Firstly you need to know the sale process to be aware of what is expected of you by the buyer, the lawyers, the buyers' mortgage company and valuer, and eventually the Notary where you will all convene to complete the sale.

Secondly, by knowing what is to be expected of the buyer and confirming that these meet your expectations, you will fill him with confidence and again create a frictionless path for him to buy.

Top Tips for getting your Power Team

- Get a team of people to help you sell your property

- You must use a lawyer

- Get a valuation of your property if you can afford it

- Get a mortgage broker to recommend to buyers who can get a mortgage based on your valuation

CHAPTER 4: HOW TO PREPARE YOUR HOME FOR SALE

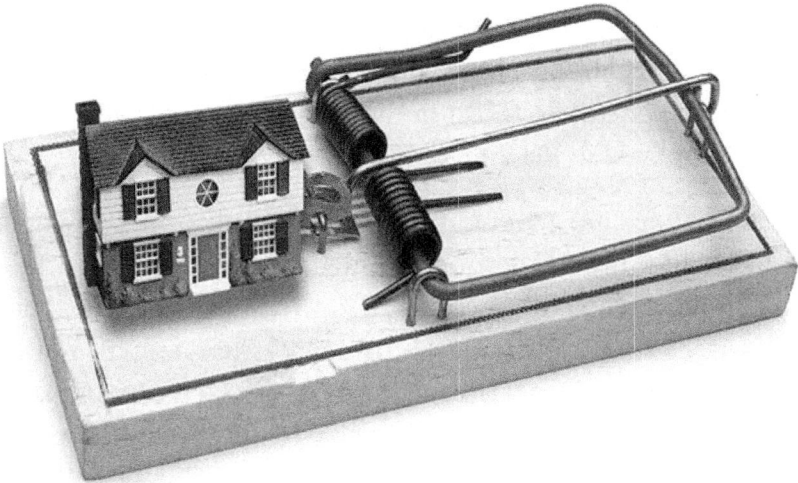

Tidy your room, aka House doctor

If you have been involved in property as long as I have, you may remember a TV program from the 80s called the house doctor, where a real estate agent gave prospective home sellers tips on how to improve the appearance of their home for sale. This program was so successful (at least in real estate circles) that the term 'House doctor your home' was able to stick and become our go-to term for improving the interior of your home in order to make it sell. If you are too young to remember this TV programme, it was a bit like 'Supernanny,' and if you are too young to remember Supernanny, then I really can't help you. The main point is that House Doctor had one very simple but important premise. Before you even think of listing your house for sale, tidy it the hell up.

This might sound amazing because it's so obvious, but you will be absolutely shocked at how many houses I've walked into as an investor or a real estate agent, which looked like the Mary Celeste. As if the occupants of the house had literally just disappeared and left everything, all the trappings of a running household exactly the way they were when they were abducted by aliens. I'm talking about clothes on the bed, clothes on the floor, and open study books in the kid's bedroom, even down to unwashed plates in the sink.

As a real estate agent, when I see this, I frown and acknowledge the disdain from my clients, apologising for having taken them to a property from which they will have to be disinfected upon leaving (I always carried a small bottle of hand sanitiser with me way before the Pandemic). But when I see this as an investor, I don't think to myself what a messy family these guys are. I think to myself, what a great bargain I'm going to get on this house. I think this because I know if they haven't taken the time to prepare the house properly for sale, then they basically don't know what they're doing, and I also know that if they haven't taken the time to prepare properly for sale, real estate clients are going to see the house as less valuable pushing down the price expectation in the seller's eyes over successive visits and making the job of getting the property at a lower price easier for me.

So let's get it right, the smarter, better presented, and more like a new development show home your house looks is directly related to how valuable it will look to the buyer. The messier or less dressed up it looks, the less valuable it will look to the buyer. This might seem overly simplistic, but this is an absolute fact. What is not a provable fact is the exact percentage this amounts to in terms of price increase or loss, but in my experience, you can add 2% as a minimum up to about 20% as a maximum to the value of your home just by taking a few measures which start off with something as simple as making it clean and tidy and looking like a show home when potential buyers come to visit and going up to more complicated things such as reorganising furniture (Feng shui, remember that), or simple cosmetic changes such as painting and decorating

Giving the whole place a lick of paint makes it appear new, fresh, and clean, and opening the windows or using subtly scented air fresheners will add to this, giving it that airy, fresh smell.

Now I appreciate that this might be hard to do if you are living in the house, and particularly hard to do if you have children or aged relatives living with you, but one of the things that you're going to have to do in terms of putting in the effort to get your home sold is to make sure that the house is at the very least tidy and presentable for when your viewings occur.

So, give the place a lick of paint. Give it a deep clean and top this up with a regular clean so it looks like a show flat rather than an in use normal home. And then, when you have a viewing in the books, make sure that you go through the house, give it another clean, and tidy everything up just before the prospective clients and agent appear. This (believe it or not) is going to have a huge effect on the price your property is actually sold for because psychologically, things that are kept in good condition are valued much more highly than things that are not. In fact, the mere fact of not taking the time and effort to keep something in good condition signals to the buyer that you do not value it or to the discerning buyer, you do not know the value of it. Even in our social lives, we see this truth. In looking for someone to date, people who take care of themselves by dressing well and keeping physically fit are seen as more attractive and, as such, more highly valued in terms of people wanting to get to know them. If I am looking for a nursery for my child and filter my options down to just two, provided all other things such as level of care, education and location are similar, I am much more likely to pay more in order to send him to the one which is cleaner and better presented. And if I am looking for a car, I will certainly see it as more attractive and valued if the car I go to see has been well taken care of.

'Hardly driven with one careful female owner, Jess was her name' is the cliché sales pitch from Honest John, the local used car dealer. But why does this pitch work, and moreover, why has it worked so well over the years that it has become a cliché? Well, you know that the car is second-hand, but although it has been used, you would prefer it to be as close to new as possible. You don't want to know that the engine is twice clocked, and the doors have been swung so often that the creaking of the hinges is an early warning that they will eminently fall off. This is why honest John will not pitch you that the car you are looking at was owned by a travelling salesman called Sterling, an ex rally driver. He drove the thing like a bat out of hell; it's a surprise that the clutch and gearbox still work. Anyway, it served him well. He was a top salesman in his region for three years running, clocking up a massive 500,000 miles from South end to Aberdeen, which is why he drove so hard and fast. Quite a success story, really, because he was homeless and living in this car when he got the job, and now he's doing so well, and this car is obviously well and truly battered; he's given it to me to sell for top dollar if I can get it.

If you think that this second sales pitch is far less likely to get the car sold than the first cliché (and I hope that you do), then don't use it to sell your house. Psychologists have for many years extolled the virtues of body language, how we communicate without speaking. The presentation of your home is its body language. It's what your house says about itself without you or the estate agent speaking on its behalf. And when it communicates on this level, you want it saying hardly used by one careful lady owner called Jess, not second-hand cast-off from Sterling.

So don't let your property fall down this very obvious and very simple to fix crack in the property sales floor. Don't be lazy, and don't make excuses. Clean your home, tidy your home, make the cosmetic repairs, give it a quick paint job, de-clutter all areas, so it looks just like the showroom in that Taylor Wimpey or Barrett's houses new development site, and if you can afford to, get a professional to do it. From cleaning to painting, maintenance, and cosmetic refurb, this is not the time for DIY, a quick and professional job is the best solution if you want to get the maximum price for your house.

So house doctor your property before putting it on the market for sale. Although the programme may well have been before your time, you have the closest thing to a time machine available at your fingertips, YouTube. So go look it up or any other TV shows, magazine articles, internet blogs, or podcasts that teach you the same process and use this information to make sure that your home is the best version of itself when prospective buyers come to call. This will genuinely affect the price you sell for. And in terms of its effect on the price, think of this in terms of securing your ability to achieve market price as opposed to leading to an increase in your house's real value. A clean, tidy house will not get you a higher than the market price, but a dirty, untidy one will get you offers well below what your property is really worth.

House Doctor your exterior

Ok, so I know your first thought when I told you to house doctor your property before putting it on the market for sale was, 'How do I do that,' so I have prepared the next two chapters to walk you through the process and point to the essential elements of the process.

House Doctor your home Part One, beautify your exterior.

The first thing that you've seen in every single property selling programme from a place in the sun through to location, location, location, or even Million dollar listing is the importance of 'curb appeal.' Curb appeal is basically your property's Wow factor from the outside.

As they approach your property, the buyer wants to get a good feeling. Take my word for it. In my years of touring property in Spain and England, I had taken potential buyers to a property only to have them stop before they got to the front gate, take one look and say,

'Not interested,' as if we were living in a horror movie and their psychic sense of foreboding had told them entering the house even just to look would mean sudden death.

I would then have to apologize to the agent waiting for me on the inside. Tell them that we could no longer continue with the appointment and go and have a drink with them to kill time until our next appointment.

I mean, come on, what else was I supposed to do. I'm there to help that buyer buy the property he wants to buy. I am there to show him the properties that he wants. Now I have in the past known that if they had got inside the house, they might have had a more balanced view. But that is really dependent on the temperament of the buyer. With some buyers, you won't even get them to that point, and let's keep it real; I'm not going to argue with the person I'm relying on to buy something so that I can make my commission. I'm not going to have a stand-down, fight with them and tell them to stop being so ridiculous or impetuous or just at least to have a look at the property because they have now wasted the time of the seller and the other agent, only to have him think what an arrogant salesman I am and walk away from viewing the rest of the properties I have lined up for that day or the rest of that week.

So actually, it's your job to get your buyer Interested, excited, and engaged so as to walk through your front door before they even get to it. This means that you need to beautify the outside of your house. I have come to loads of houses where people are just reckless with regards to how it looks outside. There were bicycles chained up outside, scruffy-looking plant plots housing dilapidated zombie-looking Triffids, knocked over their wheelie bins, people, yes people sat outside of the main window or kids toys scattered in the yard.

All of these things block the buyer's view of their dream home because the buyer has an image of what their dream home looks like when they approach it, and it looks like Nirvana. And when they enter its heaven and being forced to leave it to go to work or to the shops feels like Hell. So if when they approach your house, it looks like a building site, they're not ever going to want to enter it to see if it really is heavenly inside.

Most people just won't get over those mental hurdles, so whenever I hear myself saying anything that sounds like

'So if you can just look past the way it looks outside....' I know that I'm on a losing ticket.

So, beautify the exterior of your house. If it needs a lick of paint, suck it up and give it a lick of paint. If you can't afford to get someone to do it professionally, at least touch it up yourself so that it looks as presentable as possible. No obstructions, nuisance, or nonsense outside. No building materials, no children's toys, and no chained-up bicycles, skateboards, punching bags, or weights. If you have anything like cracks in the windows, get them sorted. Get your guttering sorted and cleaned, make sure that the leaves are off the roof, and if you can afford it, get the front walls repainted.

Ok, what else have I forgotten to mention? Oh yes.

Tidying the garden

Mow the lawn

Trim back the hedges, bushes, and trees

Clean up any animal mess (yours or others)

Clean and Mop the outside path that leads to the door

Weed all outside paths and garden areas, particularly where there is concrete

Get a professional to cover all visible cracks in walls and signs of the damp (by this mean, treat it by the way, not hide it and sell on the problem to the unsuspecting buyer)

Make sure that everything looks clean and smells nice.

Even if you don't have a garden, you can do the exact same thing to whatever aspects of the outside appearance of your home the potential buyer will see by giving it a lick of paint, tidying up, de-cluttering everything, and generally cleaning and tidying all of the outsides.

Your house needs to look like a photo from the outside; more specifically, your house needs to look like that airbrushed, photoshopped, impossible to compete with photo in the magazine they saw that made them decide to buy a new home in Spain in the first place before we even get a chance of getting them on the inside to decide if they are interested in buying it.

So don't just think that the inside of your property is important. In selling the dream, the outside visual is the first step in terms of getting the buyer engaged and eventually selling.

House doctor the exterior: Checklist

A quick list of things to check for to make sure that the exterior of your home is attractive and that your property has 'curb appeal.'

Tidying the garden (Sweep it clean and of dead leaves etc.)

Mowing the lawn

Trimming the hedges & trees, especially overhanging branches that block light

Clear leaves or pines from the roof and guttering

Making sure that everything smells nice

Removing toys, hobby material, bikes, or exercise equipment from outside of the house

Remove cars from the driveway

Put in some pot plants or hanging baskets with blooming plants and flower

Paint the exterior walls and the front door

Fix the fence and the front gate

Repaint the front gate if necessary and oil it so that it does not squeak

Redo the pointing on the front brickwork

Check window frames for damage and repair

Clean the windows and the front door

Repair any visible cracks on exterior walls

Clean up or buy new outside furniture

Remove anything old or rusty, including chairs, swings, cars

Varnish or re-paint the shed

Clean the pool if you have one

Clean and mop the outside path that leads to the door

Repair all visible cracks in walls and any damp

Repave the front drive and remove cracks

Remove all weeds from paved areas and garden areas if possible

De-cluttering all of the outside

Clean and mop the outside path that leads to the door

This is not an exhaustive list, just the things that, in my experience, have made a difference to either my impression or the impression of my clients when they approach a property.

But in terms of house doctoring the exterior of your home, if you can think of it, do it and make it look as much like a picture postcard as possible

House Doctor the Interior of your home

When preparing the Inside of your home for sale, like most things, you really need to start with the end in mind. Do a walkthrough of your home from the outside gate, through the front door, and then into all of the rooms and additional outside areas. Use a critical eye and pick up absolutely everything that might be off-putting to a potential buyer. Make a list of these things and then begin resolving them, starting with either the most off-putting thing first, or if that issue is not one you can immediately solve, then start with the ones that you can do something about right away.

Remove all elements of your personality from your home. I know it's really, really difficult for you to come to the belief that your fascination with gothic design or your beautiful Louie the 14th styled living room might not be everybody's taste, so let's look at this another way.

How many people do you know with great taste? Most people would actually conclude only a handful. But unfortunately, you're not going to be marketing your property to just a handful of people or targeting people with your own unique sense of style. You're going to be marketing your property to all of those other idiots who have absolutely no taste whatsoever. Those who don't understand that your fascination with post-war memorabilia is a thing of beauty or that your shrine to the ancient gods of Nimrod is of great religious and anthropological importance? Let's face it; they're idiots. They just won't get it. But are you here to teach them cultural refinement, or are you here to sell your house? If you want to do the first, then write a book or open an exhibition, but if your aim is to do the latter, then it's time to depersonalize your home.

Take a look at some showroom catalogues or, even better, if you can, go and visit a new build showroom. You will see that these places have practically zero personality. There are several with little flashes of very, very mundane types of art, but quite frankly, you could be in a science fiction movie or a laboratory in terms of how bland they are. But this blandness allows the buyer a blank canvas on which they can paint to their own vision, which reflects their personality and preferences. Again, as sad as it sounds, most people are just not imaginative enough to look past your personality and preferences and mentally replace them with their own. So you will have to give them a blank canvas upon which to see things their way and work out what they want to do with the space. And remember, your home is just space. I know it's home to you. I know it's where you gave birth to your daughter, where you raised your son. I know the notches on the doorposts have massive significance to you because they represent the healthy growth of your children. I know it's where you celebrated that big promotion or where you had countless barbecues and house parties which you used to embellish not just your life but the life of all your family and friends. I understand all of these things, and you will see that there is a place to share and use all of these facts in order to help secure the sale as part of rapport building which we will discuss as part of sales and negotiation later in the book. But in terms of the presentation of your property, they don't know any of that when it goes onto the market. To them, it's just space. And as something that is just space, you need to present it to them in a format that allows them to visualize how they would use it, not how you have used it in the past.

So House Doctoring does not just mean having to clean and tidy the place. It also means depersonalizing it and decluttering it so that your potential buyer can see past all of your stuff to see the space and its potential as well as seeing past your personality and how you used the space to envision the space being used as their own. Because if somebody is really against 1980's Pop memorabilia, they might find it hard to see through your home, which is full of it (both figuratively and literally), and visualize the home redone as their 25th Century futuristic Buck Rogers bachelor pad.

Finish your building work, or better yet, don't start it at all

I have already explained the need for you to have house doctored both the interior and the exterior of your house, so I am severely hoping that it is blatantly obvious and shouldn't even need mentioning that any projects that you are doing in your house on your house or to your house should be completed before advertising it for sale.

If you do not complete the project before you put your house on the market for sale, you are going to have to discount the price of your house, not only by the price of the unfinished project but probably by at least another 10%, just because they found an unfinished project sat there.

What does a project say about a house to a buyer? A project says that the house is unfinished. A project says that the house had a problem and an unfinished project says that the house has an unresolved problem. So when a buyer walks into your home and sees the unfinished building work, you are telling him that he's looking at a property that has a problem and it is still unresolved. So when you try and sell him that house, regardless of all the facts and figures you give him, if he's astute, he is going to work out that he has an unfinished problem in the property, and all he has are your word or his own builder's word as to how much it's going to cost him to have that problem fixed. But anybody who has done any kind of reformation or building knows that there are unforeseen costs and problems that usually crop up, meaning that it would be wise to budget an extra 10% of the expected cost to finish the work—an extra 10% which will have to come off your sales price.

So to make a long story short, nobody wants to pick up and finish your unfinished building project. At least nobody in the world where I come from. Nobody will take up your unfinished work.

This is not just a property phenomenon; it applies pretty universally to business as well. If you're having a web page built and you fall out with your web designer. When you go to a new one and ask her if she can finish off the half-built website, the response from most self-respecting web designers is going to be a wild resounding 'No, I can start from scratch for you. But I will not try and finish up somebody else's work.'

This is the same as an unfinished building project. Why? Well, because we don't know the standards, the planning, or the competency, to which the project had been started. So, if the project was well planned, well budgeted, and had been started competently, then it's great, and we know it can be finished as projected. But even if my builder takes a look at it, I still might find out at a later date that it hadn't been planned properly or due to something that should have been done at the initial stages but was not done, it's now actually going to cost three times as much to finish.

If so, I've now just bought myself a huge problem. So if I know enough about the potential nightmares of building renovation (myself personally or via the advice of others), I will know better than to pick up your half-finished project. It's just a no no.

Now, I appreciate this cannot be done for everybody. Circumstances may dictate that your project is stalled or you are unable to complete it, and if this is the case, my suggestions are as follows.

The first case scenario is to finish anything that you have started, even if it's to the most basic level, and make it as presentable as possible so that it doesn't have to be discussed as part of the home. Whatever the project, once it has been finished to even a rudimentary level then, It is just what it is. If the parquet floors aren't as good as you want them to be, don't make it an issue. Just say these are the parquet floors and move on. They might not know or realize how good or average they are. They definitely won't know how much better you had planned them to be. At least let's hope that they don't because if they do, they'll discount this from the price.

In most cases, buyers will not notice that you did not fit the best quality or that they are not varnished as well as they could have been. They will happily say, Well, I see you've got Parquet floors, and at the most, hmmm, they need to lick a varnish and move on. At worst, they will include that in the price that we offer as opposed to walking into a living room with half the floorboards up, only to be told that you're not going to finish it and they will have to find someone to come in and do it. I mean, just be honest. You might have decided to sell the house because when you put up the floorboards, you found termites. So, in all cases where it is possible, finish whatever you have started if you can.

If you haven't started it and you want to put your house on the market for sale, then make the decision to sell it as it is. Again, they might not even notice the problem that you see and consider in need of improvement. They might not see that the Conservatory really needs extending to be used properly. They could be a smaller family who needs less space for whom it fits perfectly, so don't start something that might not need doing because what you already have might be perfect for the person who's looking at it.

And if due to circumstance, you have to try to sell your home in the middle of a project, refurbishment, or reform, my advice is that once a buyer has shown any serious interest, you invite your builder to discuss the situation with them. Tell them that you have a builder who has been doing the project, who knows all about it, and they can talk to your builder to get a full understanding of what has been done. If they have their own builder, then have your builder talk to their builder, (yes literally arrange for my people to talk to your people 80s style) because then they will know that the project has been started and continued in the right way. This way, at least you've got the best opportunity of conveying that information with an expert talking to an expert than as a homeowner trying to get a potential buyer to take your word for it.

A meticulous buyer may want assurances based on the work that you're doing, written into the sales contract, so if it so happens that you found a particular type of very rare termite that most builders wouldn't recognize and decided to sell the house without your builder or the new buyer's knowledge, some level of security around the works can be written into the sales contract, and you can be subsequently sued for your lack of admission.

This isn't the kind of thing that everybody would do. But depending on the size of the property, it is definitely the kind of thing I would do. I mean, let's face it, why would you complain if you had nothing to hide, but if it did indeed turn out that you had something to hide, why would I not want to have myself protected.

So this is me trying to explore the circumstance from all angles. Your first port of call is very simple. Do not try and sell your house with an unfinished building project. Finish it off as best as you can and present the house like that. Secondly, don't start it at all if you're thinking of selling your house and might not be able to complete it before you plan to go to market. Put your house on the market first and see the response to your home without the renovation. Once you have had a few offers and a few estate agent comments, you will be able to decide if the hassle and cost of doing the work yourself are really worth it or if it's just better to sell the house for a lower price as a house with potential. Suppose the sales price of the unimproved home is much less than the predicted price of your home once you have done the work, then budget for the work and complete the building project before putting your house back on the market.

And in the worst-case scenario, if circumstances leave you caught short needing to sell mid-build, open the lines of communication between your contractor and the buyers and be prepared to sign assurances into the sales contract or else be prepared to reduce the piece in line with the additional risk your half-finished work now presents.

Hiring an Interior designer

Should you hire an interior designer when selling your home?

This, for me, is very much like the question of if you should do an open house.

There is, in my mind, a definitive price bracket under which it really is not worth the hassle.

If you are selling a property over 500,000 euros, then it may be worth taking a percentage of the expected sales price and hiring an interior designer to give your house that wow factor and also to show you how to open up spaces, show you how to best use your light and show you how to get or to give the best impression of your property.

How much you spend on this will depend on a number of factors, most notably the sales price of your property, how much you have to spend, how much profit you stand to make, and an assessment of the increase in the sales price that the interior design will achieve.

Just like the sales commission you pay to the real estate agent, a few percentages of the sales price of your home are well worth paying to an interior designer whose work and vision gets the thing sold, especially if it gets sold for more.

The only downside is that, unlike a real estate agent who only gets paid on results, you will need to pay for the interior design work and materials upfront, therefore, taking all of the risks in the gamble that it improves the chance of a sale.

That said, and remembering that my view on life is that everything is negotiable, you could try to negotiate a payment split with the interior designer where you pay her for the materials and a reduced fee upfront to get the work done with a percentage of the property sales price on the back end once the property is sold.

As we had already discussed, putting your homes best foot forwards in terms of presentation is essential to getting it sold so if the house benefits from the beauty and ambience of interior design as well as its external areas being sorted out nicely (tidying the garden, mowing the lawn, trimming the trees, giving it a lick of paint, tidying up, de-cluttering all of the outsides and making sure that everything smells nice), you may well get your asking price or at the very least secure a quick sale.

So if it suits the property and you can afford it, negotiate to afford it. Interior design work on your property for sale may be a great asset. You will actually get more for the property if you have had an interior designer do some work on it. However, if your property is a 150,000 euro apartment, then I really do not think the cost of an interior designer will be worth it

So what to do if your property is in the lower price bracket but you still want to benefit from the Interior design wow factor.

If your house is below a certain price, you can still benefit from the good interior design, but it would make much more sense to do it yourself because the cost is so prohibitive.

Again, this is where your house sale being your responsibility, comes in.

There is absolutely nothing stopping you from taking the time to read some good interior design magazines, going on the internet to look up interior design websites, getting in tune with the latest trends, or even doing a short interior design for property sales course.

This money that you would have spent on an Interior designer can now be spent to maybe buy a few key items or make some key changes that will have the biggest impact on the sale of your home. You can research and acquire the key pieces which will have the greatest effect when somebody is doing a walkthrough because the truth of the matter is that a completely new interior design will do a lot for your home, but using the old 80/20 rule, only a few key changes will have the biggest impact. If you take the time to learn a little bit about it, get some good advice from your friends and your realtor, you can do this yourself, saving a lot of money and getting the maximum effect from what you spend.

So at the very least, learn about current contemporary Interior design, what's hot now, what styles are in fashion, and make the few key changes that will have the biggest effect. Make the changes that will 'wow' the buyer when they first walk through your home and save the cost of an interior designer. This is the approach to take if your house is at a price point where it really isn't appropriate to pay an interior designer for their full service.

Leave your storage spaces clear

There is nothing wrong with somebody looking around your house and seeing that all the clutter has been stuffed into the cupboards, or so you might think. I mean, most buyers won't want to look through your cupboards and examine your personal items, but they will want to get an idea of what type of storage space is included with the purchase, so they might open a cupboard or two, and the last thing you want to do is make the house look cramped by having the wardrobes overflowing with items. This gives the impression that the house does not have enough space, which is the opposite of what you want to achieve. You want that showroom feel, where only 30 % of the available space is occupied, giving a feeling of openness.

I know that this is a contentious one but if you are able to leave your storage spaces clear. Do not dump all the clutter from your house into your storage spaces, thinking that it's a shortcut to tidying up the house ready for a viewing

I totally understand why you would think this is the best way to go ahead but believe it or not, your storage spaces are an attractive selling point of your home, and if someone can't see how big or useful your storage spaces are because it's jammed with all of your clutter, you have lost potential points for your home.

If every storage space in your property is full of err stuff, you are doing yourself a disservice.

So claim back that space, clear your attic, clear your Conservatory, empty half of the items out of your cupboards and wardrobes so they can see the full benefit of all the aspects of your home.

So if you have external storage space like a storeroom, then you may want to put the bulk of your non-essential items here before you start showing your property, but to be honest, the size of the storeroom that comes with the property is another attractive selling point so unfortunately, the same rule applies.

The best thing to do is to look into renting some external storage units in which to put your non-essentials until you have completed the sale in order to make sure that your house gives the best impression of space and comfort possible.

The walkthrough

So we have already dictated how important it is when showing your house to make sure that it is clean and tidy. De-clutter it so people can visualize for themselves how spaces can be used and depersonalise it so that people don't think that they're being forced to buy your 1960s Austin Powers bachelor pad.

The aim is that they see a nice blank canvas which they can work on, but there is also one more thing that you need to do, which, although related, is actually separate and removed from house doctoring your home. This is planning the walk-through.

The walk-through is the act of actually walking through your property for sale from the outside and following the route that you will guide the prospective buyers, and making a note of the obstacles, highlights, and first impressions that your planned tour will give. Once you have done this, you may well realize that you are perhaps showing the rooms in the wrong order or that some rooms need additional de-cluttering when seen as part of a tour and compared to others.

The walk-through is the art of making your property planned, prepared, and cosy for viewing and ensuring that it has the greatest amount of impact on the potential buyer.

Walk through your house as if you were the one who is going to buy it. Go across the street, look at it from across the street to get a real outside impression and perspective. Pick out the points they like or dislike and pay attention to what you think they will notice. What needs to be improved? What still needs to change? Does it have curb appeal? What did you do a great job with when you were house doctoring the external parts of your house that you will want to bring attention to when either you or the estate agent is showing your property to the prospective buyer? Once you have made a note of all of these things, it's time to go back inside.

Now walk through the house from the front door and do the same. Yes, I know that you already looked through your house when you house doctored it, but this is a chance to do it again from a new perspective. Last time you were already in it looking around, now look at it as if you had never seen it and had just come into it for the first time. What do you notice? What sticks out? What is most prevalent in the hallway, the living room, the kitchen? Is that sideboard really necessary, or does it make the hallway look cluttered? Does that Louis the 14th mirror that you were given as a present by your mother and gave a position of prominence in the living room (well, you never know when she might drop by unexpectedly) really work in the space, or does its heavyset gold frame and reflection make the room look smaller? What about the kid's school trophy cabinet that you put up because you had to put them somewhere? Does it really add value to the hallway, or does it make the passage look tight and force you to squeeze around it on the way to the kitchen?

When looking at items and aspects of your home on the walk-through, you should apply the following criteria, if it doesn't add anything, what does it take away?

Walk into your kid's rooms or the spare room. Does that peeling my little mermaid wallpaper that you put up for your daughter (when she was 6, the one that she no longer really relishes now that she is 12, but you haven't been bothered to replace yet) really give a good impression? It might if the buyer has a daughter, but what if the buyer has a son or maybe wants to use the room as a spare room or an office? It might be imposing on her vision.

So take all of these things into consideration and try to make as good a blank canvas for your home as possible. Make it look like a good quality hotel room with the rooms looking like clean, tidy, spacious, high-quality rooms so that anybody who comes to view it will be impressed with its presentation but can still use their imagination as to what they would do with it.

The walkthrough is great for this as it is based on clearing your preconceived notions about your home and what it looks like and just walking through it from start to finish with new eyes.

But even more importantly, the walkthrough is about getting a good sense of the feeling that your potential buyer will get when they come there. They won't feel good if they walk into a garden with clutter and dirt or personalised things strewn across the lawn. What you see as necessary household stuff required for an active living family, they will just see as clutter or mess. So even though you de-cluttered and packed it all into a corner or a cupboard (if you have taken my advice, you will have already removed it from the house to an external storage unit), now is the time to reassess how it really looks from an outsiders perspective and decide once and for all if it just needs to go.

I have given you a few pointers on the kind of things to look for whilst doing your walkthrough and trying to see things through the eyes of your buyer, but those are just some of the obvious ones. You know your home best, so you need to walk through it and think about what might make your buyer like this house more or less, such as bicycles in the hall, broken potted plants in the garden, presentation cabinets that block your ability to manoeuvre through open spaces, anything like that. If you are honest with yourself, clear your head and walk through your home as if you had never seen it and you will find them; yes, even after the house doctoring process, I promise you that you will find more.

So the walkthrough of your own home is super important. Here's the thing, most real estate agents won't tell you this because he either doesn't know or doesn't want to offend you and risk the possibility of you listing it with someone else. He wants to list it, so he will treat you with kid gloves and blow smoke up your ass in order to achieve it. He might tell you some other stuff later on in the process but not at the stage whilst he is pitching you for the business.

You might think that the real estate agents should have as much of a vested interest in achieving a sale as you and so should be willing to give you the bad news upfront. Well, this is true, and as much as I bang on about the bad real estate agents, good ones do exist, and this is exactly what they will do, some even refusing to list your property unless you see sense. But as I said, this is just a percentage of the agents out there, and the not-so-good estate agent with a lower moral barometer will take a different approach. As I said, he's got a lot of houses on his books, so it means less to him which of those properties sells as long as one of them does. So he can play the game of averages, listing as many properties as possible, even those which he knows are overpriced for the current market or untidy and unattractive looking because you never know, they just might sell, but as long as one of them sells, he's all good. Keep this in mind when you get no pushback or constructive criticism from the estate agent vying for your business.

I appreciate that after all of that 'house doctoring,' you might see little difference in perspective when you do the walkthrough. If you think you are not objective enough, invite a good friend, someone good enough to be honest with you, and ask them to walk through your house and point out all the things that they think will put a buyer off or if they are the more tactful type could be improved.

Also, make sure you don't just use it as an additional tidying and de-cluttering exercise. The walkthrough is about you selling your house. Which rooms do you visit, in which order, and why? Which features of the rooms and areas do you bring the buyer's attention to? Which problems or unattractive features remain which you are not going to be able to resolve before your view, and how are you going to explain? Can you balance their negative effect with alternative features? (I said alternative features people, not alternative facts). What are you actually going to say? Yes, the actual words which you will use to describe aspects and elements of the property. Make notes as you walk around and build the sales pitch up so that eventually you have a copy-written speech such as you would have if you were going to give a wedding speech or business presentation with PowerPoint. And yes, in this scenario, the PowerPoint presentation is your home, so point to the corners of your roof terrace and say,

'So if you look just here (as you point to the guttering), you will see that the terrace not only has a slight slant but additional guttering here to help expel the water. Now I know a lot of people don't believe that it rains here in Southern Spain and if it does it rains mainly on the plain, but unfortunately, that is not true. We can get quite a bit of tropical rain here in the winter months, and this extra guttering helps to get the water out much faster than other apartments meaning that we do not have the problems with condensation and dampness that some of the other properties in this area have.'

The walkthrough is your opportunity to plan your sales speech or pitch along with the order and presentation of your property to maximize its positive attributes and minimize its negative. It is your meeting prep, you practising your Ted talk, the dressed rehearsal of your stage show, and the practice run-through of your big million dollar presentation all rolled into one. So don't just do the walk-through once, do it again and change either the physical aspects of your home or what you say or maybe even the order you show the rooms until you get it right.

And once you get it right, it's time to start showing the property to prospective buyers, but it's not time to stop practising the walkthrough. As any good salesman would tell you, each property viewing you conduct is more practice of your walkthrough, and you will keep practising until you get it right. How will you know when you've got it right, you may ask? Well, your house will have sold, of course. But usually, even before this point, you may find that you do the perfect walkthrough where you get the timing and word ordering and everything right, just unfortunately to the wrong person. When this happens, do not be discouraged. Having perfected your walkthrough, you will now be safe in the knowledge that when the right person does book an appointment, you will be an expert in showing your home and ten times more likely to nail the sale

Now, as this book has been written both for sale by the owner and for sale with a real estate agent in mind, please note that the importance of the walkthrough does still apply to the latter. Once you have done your trial walkthrough once or twice and are confident with the ease at which prospective buyers can walk around your home, and you know what aspects you would highlight and how you would explain the negatives, give this information to your realtor. No sensible real estate agent (or anyone else actually) will turn down a scenario where their work has been done for them. They will not know your property as well as you do, so you giving them what you have planned and revealed during your trial walkthroughs is a gift to them as it increases their ability to sell your house and decreases the amount of work that is needed to do to achieve it. Even if they don't take all of your suggestions, they will definitely learn some things about your property which were not obvious when they listed it and will also at the very least be given some helpful ideas regarding the best way to show your house to their clients.

The walkthrough is super important, yet literally, nobody teaches home sellers to do it. Don't wait for estate agents to tell you the best way to present your home, have your own ideas based on your walkthrough. If both you and the agent are open-minded, you will find that the best solution will be found in the combination of the two.

Don't wait for buyers to tell you either. By the time the buyer has told you that you should have shown the terrace last as it's the main selling feature of your property, it would have been too late if they tell you at all. But in most cases, the buyer, and I know this as an estate agent, will just nudge their husband or wife point to something that they find distasteful or disgusting and make a mental note to mark it down as the reason they're not going to buy your home or at the least why the price is too high.

You need to go through that whole process yourself first so that you take away all the reasons that prospective buyers won't buy your home, and you make sure that the price tag seems reasonable based on the value they get as they walk through the door.

A Professional home inspection

As part of the walkthrough, you could also arrange a home inspection.

Home inspections are more commonly associated with the USA, but there is nothing wrong with using and applying the same principles to your advantage.

Like the bank valuation, the home inspection is usually organized by and on behalf of the buyer because at the end of the day; the home inspection report is the document that the buyer will use to point out any and all structural issues which pertain to your home and use as the basis of his valuation of it, so you might as well get ahead of the game and have one done yourself.

Specific home inspection companies do not exist here in Spain, but if you do not have the budget for a bank valuation from a valuation company on the bank's panel, paying a private surveyor or a builder to do a walk through and point out any potential current or future problems with your property could prove a cheaper option.

Again this could highlight things like gutters that need repairing, drainage that needs fixing, or smaller things like dampness or condensation in one of the bathrooms.

This will give you an absolutely comprehensive list of everything wrong with your home, giving you a snag list of things to fix or at least knowledge of any issues so that you can be prepared for the negotiation.

But more importantly, you'll now be aware of all of the issues that you might not have noticed without a report, ones which the buyer might notice and find important, so again, you're aware and can be prepared.

The Snag list

If you have had a version of a home inspection conducted as part of your walkthrough, you will probably be given a snag list. A snag list is a list of works usually consisting of small improvement or things which need completing or tidying up. By this point, you will have already house doctored your home inside and outside. Small improvements are to be expected here, so if major works are reported; you probably did not do the earlier sections correctly.

Once you are in receipt of this snag list, do all of the cosmetic repairs to everything on that list if possible. This is the element of attention to detail which sometimes tips a sale over the finish line

Now that your snag list has been completed, you will be able to present your house in the best light to potential buyers.

Top Tips on how to prepare your home for sale

- House Doctor your property (Interior and Exterior)

- Do a walk through to see how you have done and what you've missed

- Hire an interior designer or use interior design magazines or courses to maximise the look of your property

- Finish any outstanding building work

- Don't start any building work that will not be finished before you start viewings

- Do a snag list to sort out any outstanding issues before you view

CHAPTER 5: MARKETING YOUR PROPERTY FOR SALE

Know the market

So again, I'm sorry for any offence caused, but you want results, and I want to get them for you, so allow me to tell you what you became the moment that you put your house on the property market.

You didn't just become the seller of a house; you also became the marketer, the advertiser, the salesman, and the negotiator of it. Regardless of if you employed other people to do these things for you, the end responsibility of the completion of these tasks is yours because you are the owner of the asset, you will be the main beneficiary of the receipts from the sales, and so in the end, the responsibility of all these things will come down to you.

So here is the first thing that you need to do. You need to find out who you are selling this property to. You need to know your market.

This doesn't have to be as complicated as hiring a marketing team, although it can be, and as an agency, with a digital marketing Sister company, we do provide this service for a number of people.

But it does not have to be as complicated as the research that our digital marketing solutions arm would create. It can actually be as simple as finding out who is buying properties like yours in your area at that time.

So, where do you find this out? Well, the number one place to start is your real estate agent. How many sellers asked me as an agent the question of who's buying. Trust me, not as many as you would think. Ask the right questions, and you may be surprised when you get the answers.

At the time of writing, I have a property on the market. When I see estate agents, and I ask them, who are buying? They told me the Brits aren't coming out because of the fourteen-day quarantine, which they are required to do on return from Spain in 2020, and regardless of the price, they still want to come to Spain and see the properties before they commit. Plus, obviously, they have Brexit concerns and the same general Covid 19 concerns as everyone else.

The majority of the people out looking are the French, who at the time of writing have fewer restrictions when coming over to Spain than British Nationals and for whom Spanish property still represents real estate opportunities at very good prices.

Additionally, estate agents tell me that since the onset of Covid 19 came, a lot of potential buyers realized that property prices are probably going to fall and have decided to withdraw themselves from the market until they see where the prices land. Different people buy at different times and with different motivations. Previously, some members of Northern European countries were receiving a tax break when buying properties in other parts of Europe. Also, the prices in their native countries were extremely high, and to feed that fire, they also were experiencing negative interest rates whereby it effectively cost them money to keep their money in the bank, so any investment which gave them a decent return on their money was now an extremely attractive option.

This is the kind of stuff you need to know. You need to know who's coming to the country to buy similar properties to yours. Once you know who's coming to buy your type of property, you can start to set a plan to make your property as attractive for them as possible. What are their cultural preferences, and what is looked at with disdain? Do they like a traditional presentation or a new build clean-cut linear style presentation?

By making your property as attractive for them as possible, you will get that sale of your property regardless of current market conditions. The bottom line is that at any given time in the market, although there may be fewer people buying or selling, there will always be somebody buying or selling, and there's definitely always somebody for the right deal at the right price if marketing can be used to find them and the deal can be structured in a way that meets the requirements.

Sell your property everywhere

If you adopt the attitude that it's his job to sell your house, then you are going to put yourself at the back of the queue, and trust me, the back of the queue of estate agent's priorities is not where you want to be.

So your job is to build a positive relationship with your estate agent. Not only build a relationship with him but play your part in the sale of your property.

If you have the means, set up a website or a blog about your home.

Most definitely promote the fact that you are selling your home on your Facebook a minimum of once a week. Relate the fact that you're selling your home to your other posts; if you don't know how to do this type of stuff, contact a digital marketing agency to discuss an effective strategy of social media marketing.

Facebook is the number one place for advertising at the time of writing. It is true that currently, other new and more innovative social media platforms exist, but due to its seniority in the social media space along with its aggressive targeting and purchase of rival companies, love it or hate it, Facebook has retained its position as the number one social media platform. So as the saying goes, if you can't beat 'em, you may as well use 'em.

I mean, think about it, if you're going to take a photograph of your dinner or repost a video of dancing cats, you might as well take a photograph in your living room and talk about how wonderful it has been using it for the last four years. Oh, and throw in the fact that you're now selling your home (complete with said Living room) to move on to different things, which is why you are reminiscing about how great it has been to have had so many family meals, soirees, parties, kids birthdays and network marketing meetings there.

Also advertise on Facebook marketplace, Wallapop, eBay, as well as popular real estates portals such as Idealista, Fotocasa, Milannuncios, Zoopla, and Rightmove.

These are all great places to advertise your home for sale, but it would pay to make two types of distinct adverts as the different types of platforms will relate strongly to very different types of buyers.

The social media platforms are great places to advertise your home to people who do not like estate agencies (for one reason or another) and are looking for a property to buy directly from the seller

Some buyers will have had bad experiences with estate agents or be focused on the estate agents' commission and the fact that they can get a property for less if that commission does not have to be paid. As such, they are serious about buying a property, but they don't want to go through an Estate agency to get one because they don't want the potential for a bad estate agent to ruin the deal or to pay the estate agents fees. Even though they may know that technically in Spain, you, the seller are the one paying the estate agents fee, they will be aware that if you sell the property privately, you will be able to drop the price by 5%, the 5% that you no longer to pay the estate agent.

These people are looking on eBay, Facebook Marketplace, Gumtree, and all of the other places I listed above where properties are listed for sale privately by the owner, so you would be wise to make sure you also have your property listed there.

You want to make sure that you have a website. This can be done very cheaply by hiring somebody from a freelancing or outsourcing portal such as Upwork or Fiverr. Alternatively, if you choose to use a digital marketing company or agency to handle all of your property marketing needs, then this will almost certainly be included in the service. A one-page website or landing page to describe your property and its benefits will suffice.

You could also do this yourself without any major need for technical qualification. There are a number of very user-friendly website hosting and building platforms available such as Wix, Go Daddy, Square space, to name a few. These types of platforms allow you to buy your website domain (your www.mypropertyforsaleinmarbella.com or whatever) and then, using their easy-to-use tools, build the website yourself at a minimum cost of a few pounds per month.

If you have the time and the flare for design and copywriting, then this is a great way to go as nobody will be able to present and sell your home as well as someone who knows it like the back of their hand and has the words and visuals to back it up.

If you are not a natural designer or writer but you still want to build your own site, or you know that your skills in this area are ok, but you want this to be more effective, again you can hire a copywriter and a local photographer to go with that web designer making sure that you get the best out of the website.

This may seem like a lot of additional expense but remember that is not going to be dead money because you can also recycle this copywriting and photography if you choose to run paid ads, such as Facebook ads, Instagram, ads in LinkedIn or given to real estate agencies who deal with properties in your area.

All of these things can be quite easily done without outside assistance, although once you have calculated the overall cost of a copywriter, web designer, photographer, domain, and hosting cost with a cost put in for your time and frustration, you may well decide that paying a digital marketing agency to provide you with a done for you package works out cheaper, less stressful and gets your property on the market quicker which is key to getting the thing sold in a competitive market.

Do your own advertising.

So how do you sell your property everywhere?

So there's free advertising which is commonly known as word of mouth and social media marketing, and then there's paid advertising, and make no mistake of it, as well as the free advertising, you need to run ads to promote the fact your property is for sale.

You can still run adverts in newspapers; I would definitely put your property for sale in the classifieds because they tend to have much more effect than big-page adverts. If you use a big double-page spread for advertising that your property is for sale, you will be competing with developers who have a huge marketing budget, and that's never going to work for one single property. The big double-page spread adverts work for developers because they are selling multiple units of the same development, which makes them cost-effective, whereas the cost for a repeat advert of this size for your property will be prohibitive, meaning that you probably won't be able to run it enough times for it to be seen and registered by your target audience. Conversely, a classified advert will be effective because property hunters and deal brokers read the property section of the classified ads. Classified Ads also work in other types of publications such as periodicals, local real estate magazines, directory booklets, local papers, and any other print media. If it's local and in print, make sure that you get your property in there. Similarly, free online directories are important such as Yell.com, eBay or Gumtree, and any others that you can think of.

You will also need to move into the paid ads, which are a form of online marketing. Digital marketing is the biggest and most effective form of marketing that is currently available. Lots of businesses have experimented with running Facebook ads, but without the correct training, most people run Facebook ads very badly and waste their money. So if you're not really comfortable with the process or know what you're doing, hire a digital marketing expert to help you get the most out of your Facebook ad spend.

You do not need to spend a lot of money on Facebook ads. Companies spend easily 500 to 30,000 a month for Facebook ads depending on their acceptable cost per conversion, but all you need to do, especially when you start, is spend 20 or 30 pounds on Facebook ads to see what kind of response you get. Then based on the kind of response your ad gets, you can change it and run it again. This is what professionals do. It works for them, and it'll work for you.

If you are not proficient with Facebook ads but do not want to hire a professional digital marketing company, the best suggestion is just to make a normal post about your property. Make it as professional as you can with a series of high-quality pictures and a full description of its best points. Make the post and then 'boost' the post to your target market (Facebook boost is a quick and easy method of paying Facebook to show your post to more people making it Facebook ads without the complexity of using the Facebook Business or Ads manager). This will, at the very least, get your advert in front of a few thousand people and will often solicit comments and likes, which will give you valuable information about how people in the market perceive your property. A 4 to 7-day boost will be enough, and again, a budget of under 30 pounds should do the trick to get your property in front of enough people so that you can get a good idea of how it is seen in the marketplace and which changes or tweaks you need to do to the advert or indeed your property before you re-advertise it and get it sold.

You can also arrange to have paid ads run on other Social media platforms such as Instagram or LinkedIn and we will go into all of these avenues in greater depth later in this chapter.

Marketing Part One: Going old school

When I refer to 'old school marketing,' I am talking about marketing methods and techniques which were used before the digital age.

If you're an 'old fella' like me and have told your children what it was like having to look for a Phone box when you needed to contact somebody whilst you were outside of your home and were unable to get to your Rotary phone, you will probably know that there was such a thing as marketing that existed before the invention of the internet. If not, you are probably looking at this book quizzically thinking, 'there was a time before the Internet?' Yes, there was; Google it.

So yes, people did marketing, especially for property sales, before the existence of the digital age, and although it seems as if nothing exists if it is not on the Internet, some of these methods are still very powerful and, more importantly, very effective in getting your house sold.

I have already told you that it is your responsibility to sell your home, and these are some of the best tools that you can use to support or at least counterbalance the work being done by your real estate agent, so let's not forget these marketing tools that still exist and may still play a part.

Use local magazines, particularly house buying magazines, to get the word out.

Here in Spain, we have magazines with names like 'Home' or 'Viva.' These are magazines specifically for property listings. They're not cheap, but it may be well worth giving it a try to put your house listing in one of these, especially properties at the top end of the market. At least you know that the person who picks up one of these free Spanish Property magazines is actually actively interested in buying a Spanish home as opposed to just browsing Spanish culture or the 'What's on' section to plan their weekend. Obviously, a good proportion of the people who pick up these magazines are just dreamers and are nowhere near actually making a purchase, but the other half of the people pick up these magazines because they are seriously looking, so they will pick up anything at all related to Spanish homes in the hope that they find exactly what they are looking for. So dedicated Spanish Property magazines or Property magazines, in general, are a good place to advertise and let the people seriously interested in buying a property know that you are seriously interested in selling one.

The second level of glossy magazines we have here in Spain (Well, at least on the Costa del Sol) are Lifestyle magazines such as 'Essential' or 'Hi-Life magazine.' These magazines allow property advertising, and so advertising in them can be effective, but as they are not property specific, you will also be advertising to a lot of people who are just interested in fashion, cultural Icons, or what they can do in the area. Because these are lifestyle magazines and primarily aimed at the rich or at least the aspiration, my suggestion is to only advertise in these types of publications if you are selling a high-end property such as a luxury apartment in an exclusive area or a villa in a desirable location and it is priced below market value. This full-page ad will catch the eye of the people with the ability to buy it even if they don't need it because they will see it as a bargain which they can add to their portfolio, and as it is for sale by the owner, they will save additional money because it will not have associated real estate agent fees.

The last types of magazines that you can advertise in are the 'What's on' and 'Find a tradesmen' type magazines. These are usually A5-sized little booklets that provide information about the local area for tourists, such as bus timetables, emergency numbers, and What's on listings alongside classified lists of tradesmen and services such as Plumbers, Electricians, Curtain companies, and even beauty or massage parlours. These Magazines also accept property ads and can be useful because they are the type of things that, due to their content, everyone in the area that they serve will pick up.

Local papers can also be used. I've seen people take out full-spread adverts in local papers. I'm not sure if they are really effective because, with a local paper, you are effectively trying to crack a nut with a hammer. The buyer for your Spanish home is a very specific person, which is why the targeting features available via digital market is so much more powerful as it allows you to target the reader who will read your advert.

The targeting power of digital marketing highlights how it improved on the scattergun approach of Billboards and Newspaper ads. If you put a double-paged spread advert in a Newspaper (or even a magazine), you're advertising your specific home to hundreds of people who have no interest in it whatsoever. Most of them won't even be interested in Property; they will be there to read the local news, so in this way, only a small portion of the people who see your ad will actually be your target market of interest.

This is why you are so much better off going with digital marketing and targeting much more specifically. Like all things digital, digital marketing was designed to be an improvement of all that had gone before it and end the scattergun approach of billboards and newspaper ads with a specific targeted approach designed at making sure that only the people who would be interested in your ad actually see it. But with all that said and their failings acknowledged, local newspaper ads were always a reasonably effective method of selling property in years gone by because if the market could not be targeted to property buyers, at least they were targeted to people interested in the local area.

A note of caution, it is generally accepted amongst advertising circles that you need to run your advert eight times before it even gets noticed, which can be expensive, so make sure that the publication you use has a history and track record of successful sales from property adverts before you book.

So if you have the budget, it will never hurt to put an advert in the newspaper. I still maintain that the classifieds are the most powerful part of a newspaper to advertise property. People still look in the classifieds as part of their read just out of curiosity, and the people searching through the classifieds are much more likely to be seriously looking to buy something than somebody who just comes across your advert because it's in the centre pages of the paper even though you spent a lot of money on it. The person looking for properties for sale in the classifieds wants to buy a property, so listing your property in the classifieds will cost you a hell of a lot less money than taking out a double-paged spread and will be a hell of a lot more targeted.

Use old School flyers to reach people in your area.

Why would you put flyers out about your house? Well, believe it or not, flyers can usually be quite targeted. Just like an advert in the local press, if your house is in Malaga, you're not going to put flyers for it out in Madrid (unless the city breaks second home market was your target). You're going to put flyers out in the area in and around your home and so targeting people already in the area and possibly those who come to the area because they like it.

Again, there is still an element of trying to crack a walnut with a hammer because most of the people who see them won't be in the market to buy a new house, but even those not in the market to buy can come to your aid as you flyer will advise to them that your property is for sale and they might tell a friend.

It's not a bad thing if your neighbours know that you're selling up. Firstly they might want to buy it. Some investors like their investment property right next door. I mean, they already know that they like the road and the area; they should because they already live on it.

And even if they're not interested in buying it, they might know someone who is and get the information to them by word of mouth.

Word of mouth is probably the least leverage-able but, at the same time, the most powerful form of advertising. By that, I mean, you can put out a thousand flyers or put that advert in the classified as seen by a thousand people, but it's much harder to speak to a thousand people and tell them that you're selling your home. That said, for every person that you tell the fact that you're selling your home, or more importantly if you speak to some specific people who are well known and well connected, you can get the word out quite convincingly that you're in the market for a buyer for your home. This is multiplied particularly by telling people who will either know others who are interested in buying property, such as those who have access to groups of investors. Members of organizations such as the BNI or business and property masterminds are a great example of this. A final source of great word of mouth leverage is the hub of any community, no, not the community centre or library, I mean, of course, the pub. Make sure that the local pubs and bars know that you are selling. Tell the Publican as he is the greatest source of information for any community and if they have a board for business cards, make sure that your flyer is on it. Gossip spreads like wildfire, especially in Pubs, so this is your chance to use this readymade network to your advantage and get those motor mouths finally doing something good, telling the world that you have a great deal for sale.

Again, compared to targeted digital marketing adverts, all of this is very, very hit and miss, but the point I'm really making here is, how much could it hurt? What I've learned over the many, many years of buying and selling properties for myself and for clients is that there is nothing as frustrating as meeting somebody and telling them that you just sold your property only for them to respond that if they'd known at the time, it was on the market they could have helped you to sell it for more because they had a friend or a client who was in the market for a property in that exact same urbanisation.

In reality, you never know if anything would come of it, but it's better than not telling everyone and later kicking yourself thinking, why the hell didn't I just tell everybody I knew when I had it up for sale

So to avoid getting that feeling six months after selling your property for less than you wanted, just go out there and tell everybody you know that you're selling your property. Become the office bore, become the guy that everyone avoids at the party, make sure everybody knows that you are selling your property. Ok, I am exaggerating; you don't have to talk about it exclusively or non-stop, but just make sure you talk about it enough so that everyone and their grandmother is aware.

This way, if the question of 'does anyone know of any properties for sale on your road or Urbanisation comes up at any other point or part of their lives, the fact they do know someone, namely you, will pop into their head, and they'll be able to pass that information on, doing the person who asked the question a favour and hopefully leading to your sale.

A 'For Sale' sign.

Believe it or not, this is so important. It almost needs its own chapter. It doesn't matter how you do it, but you need to have a sign to let people know that your house is for sale.

In apartments, we put them in Windows. Obviously, for houses with gardens, we put them on the front lawn, but it really doesn't matter exactly how you get that information across. What's important is that you understand that just like everything else, it is the most obvious things that sometimes bring the best results.

It's the most obvious thing in the world for you to put a sign on the property to advertise that the property is for sale, yet so many people fail to do it. This is also frustrated on occasions by urbanisations who want to keep the facade of exclusivity and so actually try to forbid owners from putting for sale signs on the front of their own properties.

The logic from the perspective of these urbanisations makes perfect sense. Nobody wants to see for sale signs when they go to their high-cost holiday rental, and even fewer people would be interested in buying a property in an urbanisation with for sale signs, left, right, and centre. Whether you're buying or even renting the apartment; if you turn up to view the urbanisation and you see for sale signs in the majority of the windows, you are naturally going to think there's something wrong with the area, and this is probably not the best place for you to buy or even to rent.

But unfortunately, what works for the urbanisation works against you. The number of times I've made an inquiry about an apartment because I was just driving by and happened to see a sign advertising that an apartment in that urbanisation was for sale. On occasion, the inquiry has been for me and was just speculative; often, it's been for a client who I know is looking to buy in that area. On occasion, as a good realtor, I will drive around the area that my client has confirmed to me is her favourite or first choice in terms of places to buy, and even with the Multiple Listing system in place, I will still always find one or two apartments that are up for sale which I did not find on the MLS. Sometimes these properties were put up on another Multiple Listing system that I wasn't a part of. On occasion, I missed them when I searched the Multiple Listing system the first time, or on even more rare occasions, they were actually for sale direct from the owner and not on any of the systems at all. But the bottom line is that I've picked up a few properties, a few additional viewings, and on occasion a few sales, just by taking the extra time and effort to drive around the area that my clients want to buy in and look out for 'For Sale' boards.

You want this to be you. You want to make your sale happen just because you had a 'For sale' board in the window. It will mean that even though you have an agent because your agent doesn't have an exclusive contract when you sell the property yourself through this rather fortuitous circumstance, you owe them nothing; that's part of your agreement. And just for the sake of a five-pound 'For Sale' board in a window or going up to a few hundred pounds for something more decorative, such as a sign for the lawn or a banner for the roof, you have just made a sale. Remember, the proceeds from the sale will cover the cost of the 'For Sale' boards, the digital marketing, the classified ads, and everything else you paid in terms of securing the sale. This has all been budgeted for, so it does not matter which one of these marketing methods eventually achieves the sale. Yet there's something strangely and uniquely satisfying to know that even when you had done all of these other things, the sale occurred simply from the fact that you put up a notice on the property which simply said that the thing was actually for sale. Don't miss this. It can be the key to your fortune, especially if you're the kind of person most others described as lucky.

Doing an open house

You could consider doing an open house.

I am not personally a big fan of them myself, so please take this into account when reading what I have to say about them.

In my opinion, an open house is most powerful or only really applicable if you are selling a substantial property such as a villa or a very big townhouse.

A villa or a very big townhouse with a large plot makes a lot more sense to have an open house event because they will usually be priced at the higher end of the market, so make the effort of organizing an open house worthwhile.

Open houses take a lot of time, planning, and money. If you're going to do it, do it properly, and if you're going to take the time and the effort and spend the money to do it properly, you don't want to be sat there with nobody coming through the door

Open houses need their own marketing, so rather than being a form of marketing, you need to do a specific marketing project for the open house itself, making open houses a strategy that needs a marketing project in order to be a marketing project.

As I run a marketing company, I can assure you that marketing anything is a job in itself. It is a completely separate piece of work, and it is usually never easy.

So since just the marketing of the open house event itself is going to be a chore (before you even include the actual specific work of clearing the house, beautifying some areas, organizing the food and drinks, and then arranging how you're going to do the walkthrough), this only makes sense If it's a substantial property being sold for a substantial price.

In my opinion, houses priced at a minimum of 500,000 euros warrant marketing via an open house, but open houses are probably more applicable to anything selling for over a million.

The Pros and Cons of an open house

The benefits include saving time. Rather than opening yourself up to multiple viewings with new sets of people constantly coming to view the property, causing a disturbance and interrupting your daily schedule (which can become very frustrating over a long period), you can allocate a handful of time where everybody who wants to see the property has the opportunity to come and view it. This not only saves you time in terms of the number of appointments but allows you to structure your time around viewings better. You can also structure your pitch better as you will have the ability to deliver your pitch as a presentation to a group taking questions at the end as opposed to a one-on-one tour, which usually ends up at best as a conversation albeit one way for the less talkative viewers.

With an open house, you can prepare what you're going to say clearly and in advance and plan its presentation style, highlighting certain points and pointing to aspects and features as the group follows you around the house in the same way a presenter does on stage or the boardroom, drawing the attention of his audience to certain figures, diagrams or charts on his PowerPoint presentation.

Another benefit of running open houses is the fact that your house only has to be clean and tidy to presentation level for specific times as opposed to constantly ready to be seen. It is an unfortunate fact of selling a house wherein you reside that your home must be kept clean, tidy, de-cluttered, and as close to the showroom as possible at all times just in case the agent calls with a last-minute viewing. Selling your property by open house removes this annoyance as your house will only be viewed at certain times a week or month on the specific open house days removing the frustration many sellers feel of having to live in a snow globe or a shop front window until their house is sold.

This freedom to live normally and only have to put on the heirs and graces for open house days is definitely a huge benefit in terms of the comfortability, stress minimisation, and the general mental health of the seller.

There are also some very stark negotiation benefits of selling by open house. If somebody in an open house tour shows interest in the property, this has a psychological effect on the rest of the group, and it will spark the interest of others. This effect is well known in sales circles and is so known to be true that it has been used by the 'snake oil' salesmen in seminars companies who pay people to attend the seminar just to jump up and run to the back of the room pretending to sign up for offers. They employ people to do this because they know that human beings are influenced by crowd actions, and social proof in a way that some people doing a thing will encourage other people to do it too.

So yes, if you are unscrupulous, you can also use this tactic in your open home and employ a friend to walk around your property pretending to be a prospective buyer, emphasizing how nice the house is and how much they're interested in buying it in order to spike the same interest in the other people attending. Sneaky, yes. Dishonest, definitely. But is it effective? Yes, unfortunately so. Yes, people, FOMO (Fear of missing out) works.

But before you pick up the phone to 'Peggy,' your friend from the local 'Am Dram' society, to arrange for her leading role in your skullduggery ruse, allow me to explain what I mean when I say that this tactic can be effective. Firstly, anybody for whom the house is not suitable and who knows their own mind enough to be aware of this fact is not going to suddenly decide that they want a house just because somebody else does. A house is far too big a commitment for someone to buy one that they didn't really want. This level of following the crowd works better with smaller items like the 'Genius Whizz Vegetable cutter with six slicers available today only for 19.99 with a hand blender going to the first ten people who buy.'

For a high ticket item such as property, this tactic would only work for people who are already actually interested in the house and can be made more interested by the thought of a competitor taking it away from them. Loss is a very strong human emotion, so you can manipulate their fears and anxiety around thoughts of loss or missing out, FOMO as we now call it, to push procrastinating viewers into action.

But you will have to remember that for every action, there is an equal and opposite reaction, and so the same also works in the completely opposite direction. As such, even if you have decided not to use this particular nefarious selling tactic, the flip side of having an open house is that this tactic can be used against you. Negatively minded or maybe just overly astute people will be able to point out everything that is wrong in your home to the point that you wonder why they even bothered attending. And unfortunately, they will be pointing out all of these negatives to the other potential buyers. This will sometimes be because this person naturally has a negative outlook (glass half empty kind of guy), or as I said, they might just be very astute and simply pointing out all of the problems they see in order to appraise it properly and de-risk it in order to satisfy their analytical mind.

But the one you want to look out for is the professional investor who actually wants to buy the property and, because of this interest, makes a huge effort to point out all the negatives to dissuade the other potential buyers. They do this so that they can swoop back in at a later time and buy the house from you (who has now not only lost your other potential buyers due to their pointing out of your home's every fault but also been dissuaded by their negativity into thinking that you have overpriced your house), at a bargain price. They can now make a low offer and get your house for less than it is worth, for less than you wanted to accept for it.

Putting in a low-end offer isn't the problem here; investors and piss-takers fueled by one too many episodes of 'A Place in the Sun' are going to put in low offers no matter what. The big problem you're going to have is that at the open house, you have created an environment where you allowed them to dissuade the other buyers with their negativity, fake or real, and potentially lose yourself a sale.

So, in my opinion, open houses are a mixed bag. The benefits are basically based on time efficiency and the ability to live a relatively normal life in between viewings and using sales pressure and FOMO to aid sales. The negatives are losing out on viewings for people who cannot make the open house and having sales pressure used against you by Wiley professional investors downgrading the value of your property in the eyes of other buyers in order to snare themselves a deal.

So, in my opinion, there is no net gain or net loss in particular from doing an open house. The time and effort you put into advertising and organizing the open house are probably about the same as you will save by not having constant viewings of your property, so although you may not have had twenty viewings in a three month period, you would probably spend the same amount of time as those viewings just to organize, promote and run the open house if you prepare for it properly.

The potential to increase the interest of the people who attended open houses, genuinely or by your own nefarious means can equally be cancelled out and counteracted by the potential of someone else to decrease the level of interest of these same people whether this is the fruit of a genuine negative mind or their own nefarious plans.

So I think the answer to the question has to be if planning and running an open house is the kind of event that you think you would enjoy, then go ahead and do one. In fact, do more than one; run one every month until your house is sold so that you can learn from the previous ones, particularly in terms of making sure that you have the right selection of attendees.

After a few events, you should be able to get a feel for respondents and will hopefully be able to preselect the people who will have a positive effect on the open house environment and not a negative one.

An Open House Alternative

Another option that is similar to having an open house but does apply to the smaller properties such as apartments under 500,000 euros in price is to arrange viewings that clash. This is an age-old real estate selling technique and again uses the natural human psychological trait of being more attracted to something that others want or putting more effort into gaining something that we might lose.

If you run your viewings back to back, i.e., organizing the first viewing from 10 am to 10:30 am and then the second viewing from 10:20 to 10:50, you achieve two things. Firstly, you will increase the value or the importance of your home in terms of the viewer because when they arrive to see another family leaving, this tells them that for whatever reason your home is in demand, a self-evident fact because other people are looking at it. If they were to arrive at your house and it was very clear that nobody had been to see it or paid any attention to it in the last 12 months, then they will automatically devalue it in their mind as something that nobody wants.

So having somebody just leave your property as they arrive is always a good look, and if you make them wait a few minutes whilst you finish up with the previous client, it works even better. Now, if they like your home, without you even having to mention it, this factor will play on their minds. The thought that somebody else was just looking at the property, a property which they like will be ever-present to them. They will also conclude that if they like the property, then the previous people might like it too, and this will affect their decision-making. It can often spur them on to give more serious consideration to it or even into taking some sort of action quicker than they would do if they thought that there was no threat and they had all the time in the world to decide if it was what they wanted or to keep looking.

If you have the ability to magnify this by adding to the scenario a third potential buyer arriving as they leave or waiting for them as they leave in order to view, then you have now created a pincer move, a psychological vice for your potential buyer.

Again, this will not work for anybody who is not interested in your property in the first place. If they do not like the property or it isn't suitable for them, then it will make no difference if the welsh Rugby team was there before them and the Indian cricket team is waiting as they leave (other than maybe just the psychological trip of trying to work out why everyone is so interested in this property that they don't particularly think is great). But if they have a genuine interest in your home, enough so that it is shortlisted on their list of potentials, the fact that somebody has just been in to see it, and the fact that someone else is was waiting to see it as they leave will have a huge psychological effect and will be a massive motivator for them to take action If they are actually serious and in a position to do so.

If you can arrange your property viewings in this way, this will have a much greater effect on your potential buyers than an open house. What's more, it will not only protect you from the possibility of the negativity of one person in the group poisoning your ability to sell to the others but have the positive effect of pitching potential buyers against each other and leveraging FOMO without you having to say a single word.

Top Tips on Marketing your property for sale

- Do your market research to know who is buying properties like yours

- Promote the fact that you are selling your property everywhere

- Use traditional marketing methods

- Put up a for sales sign

- Advertise in the newspaper and magazine classifieds section, not on full-page spreads

CHAPTER 6: DIGITAL MARKETING YOUR PROPERTY

Digital marketing your property

The world has changed (I really hope you've noticed), I mean even before the Pandemic. Each major change is named as era an 'age' to signify its importance, and as of 1980 (according to

Google, personally I thought it started about 12 years later), we are now living in the digital age (also known as the technological age), which is onset from the industrial age which I was born into.

What does this have to do with the price and efficiency of selling your property? Well, actually, it's pretty important. Digital disruptors have affected industries of all kinds, from Print and News to Manufacturing and Transport, and now they have finally got around to disrupt the real estate and industry, which for far too many of its users have been hugely overpriced for a massively underwhelming service. Bygone are the days of 'For Sales' Signs, newspaper ads, open houses, and shop window cards being the main way to sell your property. All of these still have a place, as we have already explored in this book, but the digital age has brought with it new, exciting, and now essential methods to get the message that you have a property or sale out to the masses

Technology rattles along at a mind-boggling pace. There are still people alive who remember the world before the invention of the telephone, never less the internet, but it seems that nowadays, rather than taking decades, each new leap of technology takes years, if not months or weeks. This is definitely true of all things digital marketing so take my word for it when I say that if I were to go into a deeply convoluted explanation of how to use the major digital marketing platforms which are available to you, they would have changed their interface and moved all of the buttons and menus around making my instructions outdated well before this book was even published, (yes even if I finished the final manuscript last night).

At the time of writing, Clubhouse is taking the world by storm and is still not even available on Android phone, but I bet it will be by the time you are reading this.

So all I can sensibly do here is give you a brief overview of the main digital marketing platforms which are available to you at the time of writing and a breakdown (with no specifics) of how to use them.

For specifics, I recommend going to YouTube, the great video explainer of everything in the sky, and look for the most up to date explainer video (which actually explains stuff and isn't just a 30-minute sales pitch for a course), or alternatively, if you have the money and the interest, buy a course, a short one which avoids the need to pump itself full of filler material to elongate itself so that it seems like good value and simply delivers what you need to know in a brief, efficient manner. Or lastly (as running digital advertising can be quite complicated and definitely frustrating (Facebook Ad restricted anyone?), to people who are not comfortable with computers and technology), just hire a digital marketing company to run them for you. I would recommend Flex Gordo Digital Marketing Solutions (that's www.flexgordo.com), which gives the best service for the price. That said, I am biased; I own the company, but hey, it's my book, so I will promote them anyway. Nepotism, yes, abuse of position, yes, darn right cheeky, yep, but it's not illegal yet, is it?

OK, where to market your property online… wait… not yet, hold your horses. Before we even think about where we can advertise, we have to get clear on who we are advertising to.

Who to Target your ads towards, your Avatar

The most important part of your digital marketing is targeting. Targeting is the process of deciding who you want to see your adverts and who you do not, yes you can actually do this, and it is extremely powerful as it allows you to avoid wasting money by showing your ads to people who are not interested in buying a property, or are interested in buying a property but not in your area.

So as you probably now see, before you can target your ads, you need to know what your target looks like. Gamekeepers and Hitmen alike both need a full and clear description of their target to avoid the former shooting an endangered species they are trying to protect instead of its natural predator, which they are trying to curtail, and the latter mistakenly shooting the wife who took the hit out on her husband, instead of the husband she paid to have shot (gruesome I know, I watch too many gangster movies, but it does sort of illustrate the point). So before you try to hit a target, you need to know what it is, you need to know what it looks like, and if you are going to stalk it (whether gamekeeper or Hitman), you need to know where it can be found. This in marketing is what we call knowing your Avatar.

Your Avatar is not a Fictional film made in 2009 by James Cameron, starring Zoe Saldana and some guy nobody remembers anymore, which was basically a rip off of the last of the Mohicans, cost way too much money to make (still the most expensive movie ever made at 237 million dollars which is bizarre because it's all about fictional blue people, the Smurfs were cheaper and better, really), although there is an Avatar which fits this bill, this is not the one you are looking for.

In marketing, your Avatar is a fictional mockup of your perfect buyer. You need to imagine the perfect person to buy your property or put it another way; who would your property be perfect for? For example, if you originally bought your property 20 years ago as a 30 something-year-old young parent due to the desirable neighbourhood, its proximity to parks, schools, and other young families, then unless the area has changed, a 30 something-year-old young parent would be a great Avatar for your property marketing meaning that you can avoid wasting time and money marketing your property to retirees or buy to let investors. Now that a 30 something-year-old young parent has been chosen as your Avatar, your job of attracting them gets easier and will affect all aspects of your marketing. You will use images and videos which will appeal more to young parents than investors, perhaps pictures of young families at the local park, as opposed to business people using the apartment for travel stays, which an investor might be more attracted to. Your headline may include some keywords which will attract the attention of young parents emphasising the family-oriented aspects of the property such as 'safe, good neighbourhood, close to schools, residential.' These words will make an appearance in your marketing copy, the headline, sub-headline, and property description where you will promote these aspects of your property as opposed to words like 'below market value, strong capital growth, high yield, and above-average ROCE,' which you would use to attract an investor buyer. And finally, even your call to action will be different, as a parent of a young family may be more likely to want to talk to you in person to get a more secure feeling and personable experience than an investor who may and often does buy from a brochure, spreadsheet, and their own due diligent research.

Can you see how your Avatar affects everything you do in terms of how you advertise? I hope so because this is the key;

in terms of marketing, this is the whole enchilada, so getting this right will not only help you to avoid wasting money advertising to the wrong people but help you to find your buyer faster and find a buyer willing to pay more because they have actively been looking to buy exactly what you are selling.

Defining your Avatar is the first job you need to do, and you must do it before you move on to any other stage of this chapter because it will affect how you do everything that follows. I hope that you can now see how having a clear view of who you are trying to sell to (your Avatar) will influence everything about your online marketing, from which platforms to focus on (Instagram or Clubhouse), which images to use and which words, phrases, and key points to include in your text copy. So spend some time working out who you think is most likely and best suited to buying your property based on the property type, location, amenities, etc., and then write down the things such as pictures, images, buzz words, key facts, and incentives that would be important to and attract this person. Now you have the base information you need to sell to them, and all that's left will be the choice of platform and going through the technical motions of setting up and running the advertisement.

Ok, so now that we have our Avatar defined and written down, let's look at the platforms and how to advertise on them.

Facebook is now a necessary evil, loved and hated in equal measure but nevertheless an essential part of modern life, for now, (I have had many confrontations with Facebook over the years for their abysmal service, woeful inefficiency, and near tyrannical attitude to their power at the detriment of their customers at which points I send emails quoting 'Ozymandias' by Shelly and remind them of the demise of MySpace and Blockbuster), but I digress. If you are selling a property, for now, they are the number one social media platform which you must advertise on, so regardless of their inefficiencies and business arrogance, you cannot avoid them.

Facebook Posts

Literally, everybody and their great grandmother has a Facebook account. In fact, Facebook has become such a necessary evil in our lives that it is now also used as an Authenticator for other sites (something I strongly suggest that you do not do, because when Facebook freezes your account out of the blue for some mistaken contravention of their policies, you will also be locked out of all the accounts and sites you used Facebook as an Authenticator to log in to (have I already mentioned my professional hate for Facebook, oh, twice already, my bad. Ok then, let's get on with it).

As Facebook is 'The' social media platform of the Zeitgeist (that's a fancy way of saying era, don't you know), this luckily means that most people have already gone through the process of setting up an account and even making a post. As such, I will not go through these here; if you have not yet set up a Facebook account, I refer you to the life encyclopedia that is YouTube, where you will find a few thousand videos with examples of how to do this.

The real point of this is to point out that Facebook as a real estate tool is immensely powerful. I have seen blogs where some estate agents are suggesting moving their listings from the MLS and using Facebook alone to sell properties. I would not personally go that far yet, but since everybody and their great grandmothers are on Facebook, and their great grandmothers' cat (and Jay Z's Lips, sorry couldn't resist including that) has an account, it definitely is one of the most powerful ways of getting information to the masses. With a normal Facebook profile post, the process is simple.

Promoting your property by Facebook Post

First, you make a post promoting your property. If you do not know what it should look like or what to say about it, then go to the Facebook search bar and put real estate or property in the search bar and search for a few property companies. Look at their posts, look at the kinds of pictures they use to promote their properties (most of these will have been taken from a phone just like yours so you can easily emulate what you see), and then copy the format of the text, which will probably go something like; 'Great opportunity, two bed two bath apartment in (Town name), this luxurious mid-terraced apartment has ample living space with one large en-suite master bedroom, a good-sized second bedroom and open plan living room looking out onto the garden area. Parking space and storeroom included priced to sell; sensible offers will be considered.' (I wrote this without even thinking about it, proof that I have been in this industry for too long.)

Once you have seen a few Facebook posts promoting properties and have found a style that you like (or indeed even just copied the style of the one above), you can write out the text for your Facebook Post in word or something similar, take a photo of every room and relevant area of your property and upload them to your PC (I am by the way old school but you can, of course, do all of the above directly on your phone, oh the wonders of the modern world). Once uploaded, you can create your post, put in your text, add your pictures, post it, and then voila, just like magic, your property has been advertised and will be sold. Well... not exactly; Facebook is the monster it is because it uses the data it collects from allowing us to use it for free to sell us stuff it hopes but does not particularly care that we want or need, just as long as the advertisers keep paying. You, my property selling friend, are now an advertiser of your property, but unless you are a social media influencer, your singular post is not going to get your property sold, so on to the next step.

Boost your Facebook post

You will need to 'Boost' your post. This means paying Facebook money to show it to more people, preferably people who are actually looking for property in your area. This last point is one of contention because much has been made as to the accuracy of the targeting on Facebook. Some people and companies swear by it; on the other hand, apparently, in an internal memo, Facebook's own Execs think it's rubbish, but none the less it's still, in theory, one of the most powerful tools we have, so let's just get on with it.

Boost your post

Facebook will offer you the chance to boost your post, and you should accept it. When boosting your post, follow the advice written in the section entitled 'Facebook Targeting,' which appears later in this chapter. This is essential advice that is non-negotiable because you will be wasting your money if you pay to boost a post without it.

Facebook Ads

Before you run Facebook Ads, you will need a Facebook page. Facebook Pages are just like profiles but for businesses, organizations, or charities, basically, anything that is not in itself a human that you might want to provide information about and promote. Setting up a Facebook page is very easy; you simply log in to your profile and look at the menus until you see 'Pages,' click into pages and select 'create new' and then follow the online instructions. Use this to Create a Facebook page for the property you have for sale; yes, you can do that. Fill the page with pictures of the property, information about it, and everything that you think will help to sell it. Once your page has been created, you will see an option in a menu called 'Ads Centre.' Click on this and select 'Create Ad.' Please remember that this is a synopsis based on the rough methodology to do this today. If you need more information or if this is now out of date, you will need to Google it (unless, of course, Google is now out of date upon which you will be in a completely different epoch to me and I am afraid that I cannot help you).

Now that you have a Facebook Page for your property, you can start running Facebook ads for it. Facebook Ads are a way of allowing anybody and everybody to market their goods or services. If you have ever seen an advert in a newspaper, on a billboard, or pop up on your Facebook newsfeed in between videos of dancing cats whilst you were scrolling frantically to find that post from your ex which you pretended that you didn't care about and now want to see but can't find anymore, (never happened to you, oh ok just me then) now you have the chance to make an advert just like them. Again I apologise, but as a book on how to sell property, I am not going to go into the minutia of how to make a Facebook advert, so… it's overview time again.

The basic structure of any generic advert placed in any advertising medium is as follows;

- Headline
- Subheadline
- Copy text
- Images
- Call to actions

Luckily for you, this is how Facebook has set out its Ad building GUI (guided under interface), so you can just follow the prompts and build an advert that looks like it had been created by a pro.

What I will do here is give you a bit of advice regarding what you should aim to do with each of the sections bullet-pointed above.

Headline

Newspapers are great places to get an understanding of what a headline does, as are your notifications on your phone. If you have feeds coming in from BBC News or CNN-type sources, what you get as notification is effectively your headline.

Let me give you a few examples from notifications on my phone today (don't judge me).

Headline 'Why do so many US presidents like to say I'm Irish?' sub-headline, 'Biden isn't the only one to celebrate Irish roots

And then there's

Headline, 'How precaution may undermine public trust,' sub-headline, 'Blood clot fears over vaccines may cause long'...

Then there's

'Thief gets head stuck in railings during escape,' sub-headline, 'He was left as a sitting duck for police'...

And finally, there's

Headline, 'Blind bride to give blind groom best wedding gift,' sub-headline 'She's giving him a new vital organ,' hmmm, I think I'll save this one to read later.

The aim of a headline is to grab your attention, make you stop what you are doing, and investigate the information which follows. In terms of selling property 'Best priced apartment in an area or luxury apartment must be seen' tend to work well at getting attention but as so many agents are using these types of headline, you will need to get creative and think of your own show-stopping headlines to stop your potential buyer scrolling and make him read your ad.

Subheadline

Your sub-headline is not always essential, but when used, it is simply the end of the sentence from your headline. If your headline got them to stop scrolling, think of your subtitle or sub-headline as the bit of information that tips them over the edge from wondering if they want to read more to actually doing so. These are great places to overcome the first objection they might have about your Headline, for example

Headline

'Best priced apartment in the area.'

Subheadline

Even if you think you have seen the cheapest already

Or

Headline

Luxury apartment in the area,

Subheadline

High quality, luxurious but at amazingly affordable price

Copy Text

Your copy text is the description of what you are selling. You pretty much get this from the example I gave you of looking at other real estate agent's listings and getting ideas about what they emphasise and aspects of properties they promote. Believe it or not, this is not as important as your headline because most people have decided if they are interested or not by the time they have read your sub-headline, but like all things, we humans need sufficient information to convince ourselves that our gut reaction or decision is justified and this is where the description comes in, so make sure that it is as compelling and alluring as possible.

Images

Images are all important, whether you use photos or video. In fact, in the scale of importance, images are at the top, followed by headline, call to action, sub-headline, and then description. Why are images so important? Well, because social media platforms (with the exception of clubhouse and Podcasts) are primarily visual platforms. Even text-heavy ones like Facebook require you to read because reading is a visual activity, so with so many visual stimuli being presented to the user, your image will need to be powerful and effective enough to make them stop scrolling. It is only after the image has caught their attention that most people pay attention to the headline, and if the headline is captivating enough, they will have already decided if they want to pay more attention to the post or not. They will move on to the sub-headline and description in turn just to confirm to themselves that they are making the right decision before interacting with the advert, but if the image does not get their attention, they may not notice the advert at all, never giving any of the other information a chance for their consideration.

If you use photos, Facebook ads offer the option of a carousel, use it. Don't rely on just one image to sell a property; upload that killer image, your money shot along with 6 or 7 of your best images, and run them in carousel fashion so that the potential buyer has more to be impressed by.

An even better option is to take some video of the property and using an online video editing suite to make a short video of your property for sale and then use this. There are loads of easy-to-use online video editing tools for your computer and apps for your phone, but if you do not have the time or are not technically minded, you will also find a fair number of cheap and reliable outsourcers who can edit the video footage you took for you. Failing this, there are many companies who will come to your home and produce videos for you; these range from photographers who will also provide high-resolution video at a modest price to companies who provide high-end services such as 360 video walkthroughs. This last option can be very expensive, so as with the open houses, I only recommend it for people selling more expensive properties over and above the 500,000 euros range, although I would probably wait until I was selling something north of 750,000 before I used it myself.

Be warned that if doing this yourself, Facebook has criteria for the quality and size parameter of the images that you can upload to be used with its system. If your images fall foul of this, again, a free image editing app or tool can usually be used to edit the images to the required parameters, but on occasion, you will find that you have to change the setting on your camera and do them all again. As such, you may well want to do a trial and take a few quick pictures, go into the Facebook ad manager, and start to set up an advert to see if it accepts the images you upload. Once your trial images have been accepted, you will know that your camera settings are correct, and you will be able to go forward and take photographs of the whole house, secure in the knowledge that you are not wasting your time.

A word of caution, Facebook as a business is an overgrown out of control monstrosity, the kind which was written about in Jurassic park or Clover field. Your instinct may lead you to believe that a company this big must have rigorous processes and an efficient customer services department. I thought that too, but it doesn't. It uses AI (that's artificial intelligence to you) to make most of its judgments, the AI is often wrong, and these wrong decisions are being reviewed by humans less and less. As such, take this advice before you submit an advert. Read the Facebook rules for advertising and do not break them because if you break them continuously, Facebook will restrict your adverts or freeze your ad account. And just when you are expecting to contact customer service to get it all resolved, you will discover the ridiculously sad truth of the technological age, which is that as customers, we are taken for granted and delivered poor service at every turn. I have argued with Facebook on occasion and won, but as my good friend and Mortgage brokering associate from Manchester, Gary would say, 'doing that is about as likely as getting sh*t from a Rocking horse' so having achieved this impossible task in the past please take my word for it, it's not worth the time, headache or life force. It is better to assume the following Mantra. 'Get it right the first time and don't have your ads restricted or your Ad account banned because there is no negotiating with Facebook, ever.'

Call to Action aka CTA

Lastly, your advert needs a call to action. I say lastly, but in the above list of most to least important parts of your ad, you will see that your call to action comes third. It is amazing how many adverts are created, which are great at getting people's attention and interest to buy and then fall down when it comes to telling them clearly what to do if they want to go forwards. That is why this is more important than your subheadline because the person who is actively looking for the property in your area will already be sold on finding out more from the image and headline. At this point, she doesn't need the description or even the subheadline; she just needs you to get on with telling her what she needs to do to buy it already. OK, in reality, this is truer of small cost items than property, but the principle is the same, so once you have their attention and interest, you need to be very clear in telling them what they need to do next. What do you want them to do about the information that you are giving them? How do they get in contact with them? What are the next steps for them to be able to follow up on their interest in what they have seen in the ad?

This next step will depend entirely on what suits you and your setup best, and Facebook has lots of options to cover this. You can have a button to say 'Learn more' which sends them to your website or landing page, which has more information and a form for them to fill, which you can use to contact them and arrange a viewing. You could use a button to say 'call me' to arrange a phone call to do the same or one that allows them to contact you by your Facebook messenger account so that you can chat via text message. And finally, there is my favourite, setting up a Facebook form so that they enter their contact details directly into Facebook, allowing you to contact them via your preferred means (phone call or email) at your convenience and begin the process of finding out if your property is right for them.

There are a number of options, so make sure that in setting up the structure of your Facebook ad, you set up the option which you want to use, and more importantly, in designing your Facebook adverts, make 100% sure that it is clear what they need to do next. Have them choose the action which you will follow up on, so make sure that their inquiry ends up in a place that you actively check regularly so that you will actually see and receive their message. This may seem silly, but in the early days, I myself have run adverts that directed respondents to my Facebook messenger only to discover that I did not actually actively use messenger and so had ignored the notifications telling me that I had numerous messages from interested parties. This is important because statistics show that the sooner you contact an interested party (generally within 12 to 24 hours of their attempt to contact you), the more likely you are to sell to them. This is a general truism from a Marketing and Sales study which I am sure mainly applies to low-cost and mid-cost items as opposed to property which is a purchase that requires much more organization and thought. But however, much of it applies if you want to get your property sold quickly, and for the highest price, you cannot afford to miss out on interested parties because you took two days to answer their inquiry, losing out to your competitor who responded to them in 6 hours. This is why it is so important that you select a call to action step which delivers their inquiry to a place that you will regularly check (I mean every few hours, people). This will ensure that your advertising money and potential property sale are not lost because you were too busy, distracted, or half-assed to follow up on the interested parties who responded to your ads and might have led to a sale.

Facebook Targeting

As the targeting is now almost identical in the Facebook ads and Facebook Boost functions, I have lumped them together and given advice on how to do the targeting in the section below. This is an overview of how to target, but it is still essential. Do not run Facebook ads or even boost a Facebook post without reading it. This is non-negotiable, and if you do not follow it or something similar, you will waste your money.

In the boost and advert pages, it will offer you the opportunity to choose an audience. This is key as you will be selecting the types of people to whom Facebook will be showing your post or advert about your property for sale.

As previously mentioned, this is what separates targeted digital marketing from the scattergun approach of newspaper or billboard ads. Everyone from the property searcher to the paperboy sees the Newspaper ad, everyone walking down the street from the person who wants to buy a property just like yours to the person who thinks that buying property is a con will see your billboard, but with digital marketing, you get to choose who sees your ad, so using the previous examples, only the property searcher will see your newspaper ad and only the person who wants to buy a property like yours will see your billboard. Well, that's the theory anyway, and the targeting you select is how you do this.

This is done by looking through the options presented in the 'interests' and 'behaviours' options in the targeting section and choosing the kinds of people you think will be looking for a property like yours. Here's a hint, do not choose paper boys or people who think property ownership is a con. I could go into more detail here, but unfortunately, this is another area where I will wake up tomorrow, and Facebook will have completely rearranged everything in this section, making sure that all of my instructions are out of date, and when that happens, I will be guaranteed to get bad reviews from readers for giving out of date information.

'He said that the boost button would appear at the bottom left of the screen, but it was, in fact, at the top right; it took me hours to find it and totally, like ruined my life, dude!!!' This is the explanation for their rating of this book being one star.

So as promised, I am only going to give you the overview or, as Dick Tracey used to say, 'Just the facts Ma'am, just the facts.' If you need more detailed information, I again refer you to Google, where you can find official Facebook help pages which will walk you through the process in a way that you won't understand or for better information than the creators of the system itself can offer you, I refer you to what is in my humble opinion the second greatest invention after the Internet itself, YouTube. (They really should be paying me for all this free promotion, you know, but I don't mind doing it for free because what I say is true). If you have any difficulties with the specifics of this stuff, spend some time searching YouTube and find an explainer video from someone you understand and like; it will save you lots of time and really help you out.

Ok, so once you have completed your all-important targeting, you will need to add a budget and the length of time the advert will run. Always test your advert. Do not put a budget of 1000 euros on the first boosted post or advert you make. It might be rubbish, and you will be burning your money. You might have your audiences selected wrongly. Your advert might not be engaging. The public might be stupid and not understand what you are selling (I once ran an ad to sell a property and got five responses from people who thought it was for rent). When you first boost a post or make an advert, spend 10 euros per day for

3 to 4 days to test it. See what kind of response it gets, how much reach it gets, if the engagement is positive (thumbs up or even better love), or negative ('ha ha ha,' who is this guy and why is he laughing at all of my adverts fueling my already out of control insecurity about doing this thing which is out of my comfort zone, why dammit why?).

If after 3 to 4 days you are not happy with the results, go in and change it, then run the new amended post or ad for 3 to 4 days until you get one which gives you the results you like, and then, and only then, do you put a bigger budget behind the boosted post or advert and shoot for the stars.

Again this is an overview, there are, in fact, a lot of additional elements which go into this, and you will hear talk of CPL/CPC/ CTR/Retargeting, relevance, and audience fatigue which are all things that I am not going to go into here. They are real issues for digital marketers, and this is a book about selling your property. If you really want to deep dive into Facebook ads, then I again refer you to the fonts of free information, YouTube, Facebook Videos, Google, or a reputable digital marketing company (I think I might have recommended a really good one earlier, www.flexgordo.com or something?). As a book about selling property, the overview I have provided here is more than enough for you to muddle through and get a good enough ad up and targeted at the right people to potentially get your property sold. If it doesn't, blame Facebook, not me, they are, after all, to blame for pretty much everything else.

A final note on the design and style of your boosted posts and ads. If you really want to use this system to its maximum benefit, look on the Facebook search bar for local property companies for the ones who are promoting any properties in your urbanisation, street, or even area. If they are, I am not saying that you should plagiarise their work, but you should definitely take note of what they say and which aspects of the property or area they emphasise to give you a lead on what to put in your post to make it as effective as possible.

Final note, because Facebook owns Instagram, along with Market place, WhatsApp, and a good chunk of the so-called civilized world, you can set the adverts which you have created in Facebook to be shown on Instagram as long as you have an active Instagram account which will be a great opportunity to save time, killing two birds with one stone.

Market place

Facebook Market place is a great way of getting attention for your property. Similar to Amazon or eBay, it is a platform controlled by Facebook which will allow you to advertise your products for sale, and these can include your property.

Again use the property listing style template we have already discussed here to structure your marketplace listing. You will need a headline to capture people's attention, a sub-headline, a great description of the property to really sell its best features, and some images so that the potential buyer can see the sizes, perspectives, qualities, and those all-important views.

Instagram

A quick admission of guilt, some of the 'fanger' (that's fanatical anger, I just made up this word, by the way, let's see if we can get it into the public lexicon and eventually the dictionary, oh I can just see it now as Suzie Dent reads the lineage of 'Fanger' on Countdown 2033), which I have directed at Facebook actually belongs to Instagram. But Facebook owns them, so the hate is at least being launched in the generally right direction. In terms of problems, conflict resolution, and customer service, Facebook is bad, but at least these facilities exist. With Instagram, you have no such security. One misstep, true or perceived, will lead to your account being cancelled with zero recourse to getting it re-enacted, so again, before you even think of getting started, read the rules, terms, and conditions, particularly around advertising and make sure that you adhere to them.

Other than that, the process of setting up a profile and a business account is not sufficiently different from any of the social media accounts. The main point here is that if you already have an Instagram account, don't be shy; use it to promote the fact that you have a property for sale. Additionally, create a business account specifically to promote and sell your property and then run ads from Instagram.

As a platform, Instagram's main USP (unique selling point, aka what makes it different from the others) is that it is designed to focus on pictures and video as opposed to written text. Knowing this, if we are going to use Instagram to advertise our property for sale, we will want to focus on its visual aspects. This is the time to get a professionally made video or at the very least make a good quality homemade and edited video. Promote the property in your stories making new stories about different aspects and features of it. Show yourself enjoying it or how others could enjoy it. Show your buyer how they could live the dream.

Google

For years Google ads were the first big boy on the block in terms of digital advertising, and although they still have the most powerful infrastructure, they are no longer the best option for small-scale advertisers.

Google ads work in terms of each advertiser bidding to appear on the first page of Google (there are other pages, but the number of people who will even look at the 2nd page diminishes exponentially) when the relevant words which relate to their business of service are typed into the Google search engine. As you can imagine, with millions of inquiries and searches made every minute (3.8 million at the time of writing), the cost of getting to the top spot for a search term like 'apartment in La Cala' is, as you would imagine, huge. For a term like this, you will be competing with the big boys, and when I say the big boys, I mean Right move, Zoopla, as well as Spanish Estate agencies such as Viva Estates, Cloud nine, Bromley Homes, Taylor Wimpey Spain, all of whom I suspect have a much bigger marketing budget than you.

As such, my advice is that unless you hire a digital marketing professional to run Google ads on your behalf, avoid them. And even if you employ a professional to run them for you, beware, Google Ads are widely seen as a cash furnace within the digital marketing community, plus the returns and potential for an individual sale are much greater on Facebook anyway.

Snapchat

Once the darling of picture-loving filter using teens everywhere, a mistaken change in its interface along with the imitation of its 'Stories' feature by Instagram has forced Snapchat into near obscurity. That said, it does still exist and represents great value for money for advertisers but in terms of finding the right market to get your property sold, save yourself the time and money trying.

Tik Tok

A lot of people are busy building a branding presence on Tik Tok, secure in the knowledge that It will eventually mature and be used for business in exactly the same way that Instagram did, and though I know that this is true unless you plan to complete it on your property sale in 2034, you do not have the time to wait for this new kid on the block to grow up. Apply the last line of my advice about Snapchat and move on.

Clubhouse

Apply everything I just said about Tik Tok and move on.

Podcasts

If you get the opportunity to be a guest on a podcast and talk about the property you have for sale, do it. Make sure that you prepare using the information you have developed and the knowledge of your property gained by going through the processes in this book. Being prepared will allow you to sound informed and answer any questions that may come your way. This is the only way to use podcasts to sell your property. You could set up a podcast to sell your property, and this could be fun, and based on some of the unexpected and quirky podcasts which found success, your podcast might even become a success. But, the thing that nobody tells you about podcasts is that like all other businesses and products, they need to be tirelessly promoted for people to know that they exist and listen to them, which begs the question, why spend money advertising a podcast which only exists to advertise the fact that you have a property for sale when you can just advertise the property for sale? If your conclusion to this question is the same as mine, then you will drop the idea of starting a podcast to sell your property and just advertise your property for sale.

I hope that you have found this overview of selling your property via digital marketing useful. We have covered a lot of concepts, from basic marketing concepts which apply to marketing anything, anywhere, to digital marketing and social media platform specifics. As I repeatedly mentioned, this is an area that moves and changes at great speed, so use the principles outlined here but keep up to date with the changes (by the time you read this, Clubhouse could be a Social media Dinosaur) and use current explainer videos on YouTube or any other such platform to learn how to use the latest versions of the interfaces

Top Tips to Digital Marketing your property for sale

- Find your Avatar

- Pay a professional if you want to run Google Ads

- Do Facebook posts about your property sale and then use the 'Boost feature' to advertise it

- Run Facebook Ads

- Do not get drawn into using other social media

CHAPTER 7: WORKING WITH ESTATE AGENTS

Choosing a real estate agent Part 1: What to look for

I covered this at length in terms of what a buyer needs to do when choosing an estate agent in my book 'How to buy property in Spain', and most of this advice applies exactly the same to a seller. The main point to remember is that almost all agents will be using the Multiple Listing System, so the end agent who brings the buyer to your house may not be the one you personally listed it with.

That said, the person you've listed with does play a pivotal role, so you need to make sure that this person is honest, open, hard-working, has a track record of selling in the area, and, more specifically, has a track record of selling properties like yours.

For example, if you have a 3.2 million euro villa, don't list it with an agent who specialises in selling two-bed, two-bath apartments. It doesn't mean they're not going to sell it, but there will be agents who specialise in villas, and they will have the kind of database of villa buyers, have the digital marketing budget to get the villa promoted on the right websites, advertise in the high life luxury magazines where people who want to buy villas look, so they're gonna have a much greater probability of getting that type of property sold.

So when it comes to interviewing a real estate agent, ask them questions about their business. Try to get a feel more than anything else for their attitude and their approach. This is difficult because lots of people are great at selling themselves even though they're telling you a bunch of lies.

As with most things, you will also need to get referrals, references and look for reviews. Go to all the usual places that you get reviews, such as Facebook and Trust pilot, to see if they have any, and failing this, Google, the company and see what has been said about it elsewhere online. Ask them directly if they have reviews, testimonials or if they have referrals from other people who have used them and then follow up and contact these people to make sure that the reviews are real, make sure that they actually got the level of service that the agents promise you.

If you do nothing else in this book, do this because it's possible that your agent is going to be taking the lion's share of the responsibility to sell your house, and if you're going to give the listing to them, then you're going to need to make sure you've given it to the best one that suits your purposes as well as the one who is open to your own efforts to sell the house as well.

Choosing a real estate agent Part 2: What's in it for me?

What's in it for me?

This is the question that everybody who has ever been asked to do anything has asked since the dawn of time. It is the cornerstone of early human interaction systems such as barter and the reason for the formulation of systems to simplify them, which we commonly call money. Because we now have a system called money. What's in it for me seems to be overly simplistically. When the listing contract is signed, you it tells the real estate agent what they're getting financially in recompense for selling your home, very clearly, telling him what's in it for him if he manages to sell your property.

So, yes, of course, the real estate agent will do the work for money, but she will also have other motivations too. Just like the buyer, your real estate agent's other hot buttons must be pushed if you want to get to the top of their scale of importance. If you want to be in the top five properties that they are trying their hardest to sell, you will need to look to these motivations as well.

Prestige can be a motivation, is there's anything prestigious about your home that they could be excited about? If there is, make sure that she knows that so that she knows she is part of a prestigious sale and has something that she can brag about to other people regarding your sale other than the commission she got for it. Also, if you are a prestigious person and you can spread the word of how she sold your house to others who might want to give them business, make sure they know this too; just don't be too gregarious with the name dropping. Let me assure you that almost every client everywhere tells you about the hoards to new business waiting to be unleashed on you by mere association with them once you have done a great job for them (and usually at a discount). It is one of the great business lies and extremely powerful because you never know. Once you have been in business as long as I have, you neither believe these promises nor care if they are true. Simply doing your job well and being paid your value for the work you have performed is enough. So don't lie about it; this makes you as transparent as the real estate agent who promised you 35% above the market price if you listed the property with him. But if you are well connected and genuinely can tell other people about his service or will give them referrals, you might want to use this as a hook to secure the importance of your property in her mind. I mean, who doesn't want more business.

Also, believe it or not, even in the 'cut your Granny's legs off to make a few more quid in commission' world of real estate agency, there are some genuine people who actually like to know that have helped people. So if the reason that you're selling your home is that you need money to help your grandkids or due to the fact that you have to relocate because of illness, make sure they know this. There's nothing wrong with invoking a little bit of compassion to push you up the scale of their list of importance. In addition, they will also tell the potential buyers evoking their compassion and willingness to help. This doesn't mean that they are going to buy your house when they don't like it just because they want to help you out, but it will mean that they will see another dimension to you as a home seller, not just another faceless person selling a house but a real person with real objectives and motivations. This means that you become more real in their mind and therefore more memorable to them well. In sales, we have a saying that Stories sell. So let the estate agent know your story and use it to get them to build rapport and empathy with not just you but your home.

Make friends with your estate agent

Obvious, right, yet so few people do this. It's much more usual for people to pick up the phone and scream at their estate agent. It is much more likely for a seller to call their agent and fume...

'Why haven't I had any viewings? You've had my property for four weeks now and nothing....'

Than for him to pick up the phone and say,

'Hey, how is everything going? I noticed that you have not managed to get me any viewings. I understand that the market is slow at the moment, and I really appreciate that, so I just wanted you to know that I've just done 'this or that' to improve the value of my house or the offer.'

Maybe this will help your estate agent and motivate him more than threats to go to the competition.

Remember, your estate agent is your partner, not your adversary. Buy them doughnuts. Yes, pop into the office bring them a coffee and a cake. Make yourself memorable. This might seem horrible to some people, but it works. You want to be memorable. You want to be the person they remember when I hear about a buyer who might be interested in a house just like yours. You don't want to be the person that they are trying to forget about, or even worse, remember, but remember with animosity and disdain.

Selling with a Real Estate Agent

As I said right at the start, this is not a 'For sale by owner' (also known as FSBO) book. This is a get your property sold as quickly as possible for the maximum amount that you can get for it book. As such, the aim here is not to teach you how to avoid working with real estate agents. In my opinion, not working with estate agents would be a massive error. Such a decision is usually based on a dislike of real estate agents, possibly from previous bad experience, a want to save the commission payable to them if they sell your property, or worst of all, driven by the ego-born incentive of doing it yourself. These are all valid reasons, and if they are important enough to you to potentially lose thousands of pounds on your property sale or add months to the time it takes to find a buyer, then, by all means, sell your property FSBO. But if you want to sell your property quickly and maximise the sales price, then you are going to need to employ every tool in your armoury, and real estate agents are a pretty big and effective tool whether you like them or not. In terms of an army going into battle, you might think of them as the Goliath sized warrior with bad habits, a bad attitude who does not care about the kingdom or his fellow warriors and is really only in it for himself; but he is such a strong, skilled and powerful warrior that as long as he can be paid to fight on your side, it still makes sense to work with him and definitely better to have him on your side than against you (hmm that sounded very Game of Thrones).

I'm not knocking real estate agents (well, not much). As I pointed out before, there are some extremely good ones to whom none of my many criticisms applies, but just like in any other business, there are some extremely bad ones, and the disasters caused by this handful of scoundrels, unfortunately, makes more noise than the good deeds of all the others put together.

More importantly, whether the agent you engage in selling your property is brilliant, distinctly average, or utterly crap, as I mentioned before, the real problem you have when faced with selling your property via an estate agent is the real issue of making your property a priority for your agent. Put Frankly; your number one problem is trying to find a way to get your real estate agent to give a **** (please introduce your four-lettered profane word of preference based on your own sensibilities). Personally, I was going to say 'damn' and find some of your suggestions quite shocking...

As I pointed out before, your real estate agent will have a multitude of listings on his books directly from other local sellers who have given him the job of selling their property. Add to this the properties which he has available to sell from the Multiple Listing System, and it is easy to see that even in terms of getting the attention to your listing, your property has competition. He has lots of other properties which he could sell and will, for obvious business reasons, focus on the one which he thinks that he can sell most quickly or for the most money, meaning that unless your property is the quickest potential sale on his books or paying him the most in commission, your home is not going to be a big priority.

Suppose you're using a real estate agent; never underestimate the power of rapport. Put simply; you need to make these people your friends. First of all, you need to make them notice you, and then once noticed, you need to make them like you. This might feel like advice from a 1990s high school teen drama, and that is fine because the comparison is the same, just like the new kid in school, you want to be noticed for the right reasons, and you are competing against all the other well-established groups who already have their connections to find your a place in their environment and make yourself matter. So an aloof 'Do the job I'm paying you for' attitude will not be as effective as you might like or expect it to be. I made clear in the sister book to this 'How to buy a property in Spain' that estate agents essentially work for themselves, not the buyer or the seller, even though in Spain you, the seller, is the person paying them. So when you adopt the attitude of doing your job, you are essentially telling them to look after their own interests. Yes, I know this seems crazy based on the fact that you are paying them to sell your property, but as I said, so is everyone else on their books, and their primary job is to sell as much as they can as easily as they can, so getting the best from your estate agent will require a little more nuance.

You need to make the selling agent your friend. This is a trick that buyers use, but sellers never do. You need to pop in and see how they're doing. Take them doughnuts; maybe take them out of the office for a cup of coffee (yes, I know I have said this before, but estate agents like doughnuts, in fact, some estate agents are doughnuts, sorry I couldn't resist). Now admittedly, the sales agent is much less likely to do this because you are only a seller, who in most cases represents one sale, as opposed to a buyer who can often represent multiple sales, but you should at least try. The greater impression you can make on them is the more likely your property is going to come up in their thoughts when a potential buyer comes through the door, and if they like you, they are more likely to push that little bit harder on your sale than other listings for which they have no relationship with the owner. That's why it's worth your while to try to build some rapport; treating them as a servant will not bring you the results that you want; treating them like a friend will.

In terms of influencing your real estate agent, other than rapport, we still have the number one incentive maker at our disposal. The most powerful motivator in business since the dawn of time, which, whether said explicitly or implicitly, is always inferred. What's in it for me? Also known as paying me more money.

Pay your agent more. If you've just put your property on the market, you might not see the value of this strategy because having just put it on the market; you might be able to sell it for a price that you are happy with whilst paying the minimum amount to the estate agent (indeed we discuss strategies to do just this later in this book). But if your property is still on the market nine months later whilst other people have sold similar properties in your urbanisation or on your street during the same time period, you might look back decide that this wasn't a great choice. You really need to look at the opportunity costs. You need to assess the extra money that you are willing to pay the agent for a quick sale set against the running costs that you will have to pay to keep the property if it takes longer to sell without this extra incentive.

Let's say, for example, you are selling a property for 100,000 euros, and the normal real estate agent's fee is 5% for sale. Let us also assume that all things being equal, a property such as yours takes on average six months to secure a sale. The difference to you in terms of costs to pay your estate agent, 7%, as opposed to 5% on the 100,000 euro property, is the extra 2% which equates to another 2000 euros. Assuming as I have been suggesting that in terms of the real estate agent's efforts, a higher commission will secure more of his efforts leading to a quicker sale. Then, for example, if an agreed commission of 7% would secure the sale of your property six months faster than offering the standard 5%, the question to ask yourself is,

'Is it worth spending an additional 2000 euros in costs to sell my property quickly?'

In answering this, you will need to look at the running costs of the property. You will need to look at how much it will cost you in additional Community fees, Mortgage payments, loss of rental (it is unadvisable to rent a property out whilst it is up for sale), government rates, and other maintenance fees. Let's say, for example, all of these things cost you 6,800 euros per year, meaning that they cost you an additional 3,400 euros every six months. If your property stays in the market for another six months, it is very likely that it will conservatively cost you more than 2000 pounds, and most importantly, in most cases, you can't just put the price up. You can't say every six months that since the property has cost me another 3400 euros to own, I'm putting the price up to recoup that additional cost. You cannot do this because (staying with the example of the 100,000 euros property you have for sale) if the property did not sell for 100,000 euros in the previous six months, it is not going to sell for 103,400 six months later or 106,800 in 12 months time. If your property is not selling, you are more likely to have to put the price down, not up.

Whereas if you incentivise your agent by offering him more money to sell your property, he will almost certainly put more effort into selling your property than the other 10,000 listings he has access to and if he is indeed successful in selling the property within a six month period, rather than having spent more to sell the property, you will have in fact spent less.

And most importantly, if your agent doesn't sell the property, you will never have to pay the higher 7%, so this isn't money that you're spending; this is money that you're offering to incentivise him to try harder to sell your property. It does not stop you from following the other FSBO advice in this book, potentially selling it yourself, and not having to pay any agents anything. But if your estate agent does sell your property at an above-average speed, then you will be making a saving on the 1400 euros (the 3,400 euros it would cost you to keep the property for an additional six months minus the extra 2000 euros you paid the estate agent to incentivize the speedy sale) more than sellers who wait for the average time for their property to sell.

So go old school, offer your real estate agent more commission for a quick sale. If you don't want to give him an extra percentage, offer him a bonus and have it written into the listings contract. Write down with the company that you will pay an extra 500 euros, 6000 euros, whatever you're comfortable with, and it makes sense economically if they sell the property within a certain space of time or at a certain price.

As part of this negotiation, make sure that you have a very frank conversation with them with regards to what they actually think they can sell your property for. The fact that you are offering them a bonus to do it should help to focus their attention and separate you from the plethora of other sellers they have contracts with. It should enable them to cut the crap and abandon the usual strategy of giving you a price that will make you happy to sign your property on their books just to enable them to have another card to put in the shop window. They can now earn more money for selling your property, for actually doing the job and doing it quickly, so it is in their interest to level with you and tell you the price that they honestly believe your property can be sold for. If they are honest with you and their suggested price fits with your financial constraints, then you can sell your property faster, saving you money by paying them more.

Unfortunately, not every seller will be able to accept this realistic quick sales price. So if you really just need to get out, but the price which he gives for a guaranteed sale is less than you can afford to sell for, at least you now know the reality of your situation and can reassess your options. You can still give it to him to sell, but forget the incentive, just offer the standard 5% commission and leave your property on the market at the higher price crossing your fingers that you get lucky and he sells it at that price (but knowing what your property can and will sell for if your circumstances worsen and it comes to an emergency).

Another option would be to hedge your bets and set up a graded payment system. This type of system doesn't have to be complicated at all; it can be very simple. You can make him an offer such as; If he sells it for the full asking price, then you will pay him 7% in commission, if he sells it for the average market price, then you will pay him the standard 5%, and if you take an offer below the average market price, then a reduced commission of 3.5% is payable.

This type of graded commission system will incentivise your real estate agent to firstly look for the people who will buy your property at your full asking price. Then failing that, secondly, at the very least see if they can find somebody who buys it for the average market price and if all else fails, they still have a way of earning money from selling it for less than the average price, but if they do this part of the loss you make will be offset by the fact that you now pay them less than market commission.

This will create an incentive for them to not be lazy and to avoid bringing people in to put stupid low offers on the table. It will help you to avoid the real estate agent bringing their investor friends over to do a quick deal on your property, people who are buying for investment and as such are going to offer you 35% below market value. They won't waste your time with these people (at least initially) because they're not going to want to sell to them and earn the lowest potential commission. They are going to try to find buyers at the higher part of their commission scale, only dropping down to the next level when they have completely exhausted all opportunities in the higher ones.

As a seller, this is a power in your hands which most sellers are unaware of because they do not approach the sale of their property like a business offering incentives and penalties to the service providers they employ. Now, I must be clear that not every estate agent will agree to this type of graded commission scheme, which is fine because you do not want to deal with the inflexible and backwards-thinking estate agents anyway. The open-minded and dynamic ones are the ones most likely to get your property sold, so you are going to go for the estate agents who are willing to be flexible. Yes, we might be in a recession; yes, everyone in the world is trying to sell their properties, yes, you have to be realistic with your prices, but that doesn't mean that you are powerless in the process. This is a great way for you to exercise your power and get what you want or at least something close to what you want regardless of the external circumstances.

Different kinds of listing contract

Following on from a point I just alluded to, there are all kinds of listing contracts. No, you do not have to just sign whatever piece of paper the estate agent puts in front of you when giving your property to a real estate agent to sell.

Real estate agents can vary between companies, organisational types and definitely vary between countries. For example,

Americans have to be certified as realtors to work in their profession, whereas, in the UK and Spain, anybody with a mobile phone, a car, and a bit of blag can be a real estate agent.

Just as there are all types of real estate agents, there are also all kinds of listing contracts. The point I make to every single business or consumer is that absolutely everything is negotiable, so don't allow the real estate agent to convince you that his contract is the only listing contract available, and the terms and conditions in his listing contract are the way it has to be.

The only people who have any say in terms of what your listing contract can and cannot include are the courts and the government, so outside of breaking the law, the listing contract can look anyway, which the two of you agree.

Now obviously, a lot of agents won't agree to make changes to their standard listing contract for the simple reason that in order for them to work efficiently, they will need to be able to work to some kind of a standardised process which allows not just them but their staff to also be able to work and to delegate.

So, I'm not going to suggest that you try to get a completely new and unique listing contract arranged, just for you and your property. What I am suggesting and what definitely can be done is making amendments to clauses which you don't like, changing disadvantageous things which can be removed, and adding the things that are important to you which can be put in.

I think the most important part of the listing contract is that it is non-exclusive. A non-exclusive contract allows you to give your property for sale to more than one estate agent at the same time so that you don't restrict your ability to sell to just one agent, but you can have more than one agent working on it. This gives you the freedom and flexibility to know that if one agent is performing badly you are not stuck with him or his 'piss poor' performance as the others may be performing well. (Actually, with the MLS system even if you sign a non exclusive contract with your agent, it is still best to do your research, find a good agent and give your property to one agent at a time, something I will explain more later in this chapter)

Second in importance is that it is time-bound, a year would be my maximum, but personally, I would have it reviewed every three months because if the agent hasn't shown me that they're actually trying to sell my property in three months, I'm going to give that opportunity to another agent.

And lastly, even if you pay a fee to list the property to cover the agent's administration costs, it is important that this is all that you pay them unless they are instrumental in the eventual sale. Even if it's on their book and in their shop window, if you sell it yourself, you pay them nothing, or at the very most, you pay them a minimal fee to cover the remainder of their administration but nothing in terms of a percentage of the sales price. This way, the agent will be aware that even if you've given her the exclusivity of marketing on the MLS system (which might make her lazy and just sit around waiting for other MLS agents to find your property and provide her with the buyer), she isn't completely out the woods and working without competition because you might sell the property yourself, and if you do, she has no money coming.

I mean, why the hell would you pay her a penny? As I have been a real estate agent, I know how much work goes into marketing and following up with prospective buyers for a listing, but unfortunately, in business, results are all that matter and money talks, so no matter how much they spend on the marketing, if they don't sell it, you don't owe them anything (this is why it is so abominable to try to go behind their backs and sell to a buyer they found without paying them their dues). Now If you want to be charitable and amiable about this (this is a choice, not an obligation), you can pay her a nominal fee, a flat fee for having had it listed, and for the administration work involved in having the property listed for you, getting it on the relevant systems, her attempts to market it and sell it and the costs incurred in arranging and conducting viewings of the property. But at the end of the day, no matter what people would like to have you believe, in the real world of business, people are paid on results, and if she didn't put sufficient work in to get the result of selling your property, then there really is nothing to pay her for. This is the risk that estate agents take; it's an acceptable part of the business, it is one of the reasons they leverage systems like the MLS, it is the reason they charge a high percentage (because one successful sale has to cover the cost of many other failures). For them, this type of loss is expected and budgeted for, so if you list it with them and they do not sell it, they are not expecting any money, and so your conscience should be clean, especially if you put in the time and effort and sold the property yourself. So this has to be very clear in the contract that if you sell the property yourself, she gets paid nothing.

There may be some other things you want in the listings contract as well. For example, if she gets a reservation on the property and then the potential buyer pulls out, you will be within your legal and, in my opinion, moral right to keep the reservation fee.

What happens with this money is another thing that you might also want to be covered in the listing contract. Legally all of this money goes to you, the seller because you are the one who took the property off the market at reservation, so you are the injured party in terms of a loss in opportunity costs from the buyer pulling out of the sale. That said, many estate agents would want a share of this reservation fee, and almost all estate agents will want to be paid their fee if the buyer pulls out after exchange at a private contract. If all of this money goes to you, or if any part of it is shared with the estate agent, are all things that are worthwhile making clear and in writing.

Now you are going to piss off your listing agent because most sellers will just pitch up, scribble away at whatever the agent puts under the nose, and then leave them to it. That's fine because most of the people they are dealing with haven't read this book. Most of the people she's dealing with will not have been four armed with a complete strategy on how they might even sell the property themselves, even though they use the listing agent. But luckily, you are not most people. Most people are going to sit there with their property stuck on the market for much longer than it needs to be, wasting a lot of money maintaining the property and paying the fees and taxes on a property that they can't sell until they eventually sell the property for much less than they wanted to. But, I repeat, having read this book, you are no longer most people. Armed with the tools and strategies in this book, you don't plan to do any of these things, so you are not one of her 'most people' clients. You have every right to negotiate in terms of the listing contract you want. That's the beauty of business, trade, capitalism, and democracy. Nothing is set in stone, and just because that's the way most people do it certainly doesn't mean it's the way that everyone has to do it.

If he disagrees, ask him if he uses an iPhone. If he does, then remind him that if Steve Jobs had thought the way he thinks now, he wouldn't have anything to make his phone calls on, listen to his podcasts, or use any of the applications that are developed based around the fact that iPhone did things in a way that nobody else did.

Make sure the listings contract works for you. A non exclusive contract does not mean that you have to give your property to multiple agents, just that you have the legal right to. Giving your property to multiple agents usually just leads to multiple listings on the MLS. Now there is nothing wrong with duplicate listings (if that particular MLS system allows it), but if you find an estate agent that you trust and get a contract that you are happy with (especially if you are going to game the system the way I suggest), then I really don't see the point. If you are going to use multiple agents at the same time, use one agent from each different MLS system such as one from Resales Online and one from Infocasa, or use some who are part of an MLS and some who are not.

Also, on the MLS system, it doesn't always look good when three or four agencies are promoting the same property. As an agent representing a buyer, to me, is a sign of desperation on the side of the seller and an indication of a possible opportunity to exploit

So in terms of choosing an estate agent, take your time to choose the best one, one who will agree to the terms which suit you the best. If there are four or five other estate agents on your local high street, nothing is going to stop them from selling your property once you have made your selection because it will probably be in the MLS system for them to access and promote it to their database. So other agents can always jump in and promote your property once it's been uploaded, ready for sale, and send it to their potential buyers with the aim of getting the property sold for half of the Commission payable. And as I said before, if the agent that you gave it to doesn't perform to your expectations, if they are not putting in the effort or showing you that they are getting results, then based on the clauses which we suggest you have in the contract, you can have her replaced within three months but more importantly because your contract is non exclusive you can begin working with another estate agent immediatley, moving your listing on to the next agent on the high road to see if they do a better job.

The MLS system 1: What it is and why you should join it

Previously I have spoken about the MLS system. So now it is time to explore this backbone of modern real estate and explain to you how you can use it to your advantage when negotiating with a real estate agent.

Almost every country or region has some version of the MLS system. The MLS system is, in short, a multi-listing system. It is a database that estate agents pay to join where they can list their properties and have them sold by other agents. The aim of the MLS system is to create a resource that estate agents can use to not only find properties to sell, which they did not list themselves but promote properties which they have listed but cannot find a buyer for to other estate agents who may have buyers for these properties. If another estate agent has the buyer on his books who goes forward and buys the property that the listing agent has for sale, then they share the commission (usually but not exclusively in the ratio of 50% each).

So now that you know what it is, your next task is to find the most popular one in your area. In my region of Andalucía, the main MLS systems are Resale's online and Infocasa.

So in understanding how the MLS system works, when you put your home up for sale, you will contact a local estate agency in order for them to come around to your property, take some photos and an inventory of its size, dimensions, main selling features and price in order for them to market your property for sale (the listing). Once listed, they will summarise the main points of your property and usually print them out onto an A5-sized card (a window card), which they put in the window of their office where they advertise all of the properties which they have for sale.

But this is not the end of the story. Most estate agents will also digitally transfer that window card information onto the MLS system of which they are a member. For the estate agent, this is a way of hedging his bets. He might find you a buyer through his own resources and make 100% of the sales commission (a risky business strategy which we will look at later in this chapter), but he is better off hedging his bets and adding the might of all of the other agents in the MLS system to his sales team, allowing them to see that your property is for sale and hoping that one of them has a potential buyer looking for a property just like yours through whom he can sell your property and share the sales commission.

If he is indeed successful in this endeavour, he won't actually be the agency to find the buyer, although you listed the property with him. Another estate agent will find the buyer, and when the sale is completed, and you pay the estate agent his 5% fee, he will split this money 2.5% each with the agent who brought the buyer to the table.

So, if you'd like to save yourself 2.5% on the price of selling your home, join the Multiple Listing system yourself for a six month period because as long as the price of joining the Multiple Listing system for six months is less than 2.5% of your property sales price, you are going to save money. Specifically, you will save 2.5%, which you would have paid to the local agent for just putting the details of your property on the database.

Here is a quick example for clarity

Let's say that your property is reasonably priced at 100,000 euros. Based on the standard 5% sales commission, you will pay 5,000 euros to the agent (or agents) involved when your property is sold. Now, if the listing agent sells the property solely through his own network or hard work and diligence, then he will earn all of this money for himself, and it will be well earned. But if he puts it on the MLS system and sells it through another agent (then even if he marketed it himself as well), the fact remains that his contribution to the resultant sale, was in reality, simply writing down the details of your property and uploading them to the database so that another agent could match it to a buyer.

As such, regardless of how much effort he himself made in trying to achieve a sale, if it is eventually sold through another agent on the MLS, in terms of value, 2,500 euros (2.5%) of the full 5,000 euros sales commission is a lot of money to pay him for just uploading the particulars of your property to a database so that another agent could see it and match it to a buyer. Sorry local estate agent, this may seem harsh, but it is true.

So going back to the numbers, let's say that membership of the MLS system costs 200 euros a month. Using 'some quick maths' (Roadman shack pun intended) will show us that for the same cost as paying the local estate agent to upload your property to the system (the 2,500 euros he will earn if another agent sells it), we can divide that by the monthly cost of membership =2500/200 and discover that we could indeed pay to be a member of the MLS system ourselves for 12 and a half months with what we pay him just to upload our property to the database. Let's say we are not very technical, and so we pay someone 100 euros to upload the property details and pictures to the MLS system on our behalf. This still gives us 12 months access to the system and all of the other agents (and their potential buyers) on it for a whole year for the same amount as we would pay the local agent if we allowed him to list it and put it on the MLS system on our behalf

Now once our property has been self-listed on the MLS system, how much will you save? Well, as you would imagine, that depends on how long it takes to sell. If we sold it within six months of listing, we would have saved an amazing 1,250 euros in sales costs. If we sold it quicker, let's say within three months, we would have saved a whopping 1,900 on sales costs. If your property was priced well enough to sell straight away, you would save 2,300 euros in sales costs, and even if your property took 11 months to sell, you would still save a couple of hundred euros, so still no loss. Your only risk appears if your property fails to sell at all, but if you follow the instructions and suggestions in this book, that should not happen.

I appreciate that these savings may not look gigantic, but in terms of the small amount of effort and hassle required to list your property on the MLS yourself, they represent a great return on your time and effort. And most importantly, as the MLS membership is a flat fee cost, not a percentage of your property's sales price, your savings increase exponentially with the sales price of your property. So, for example, if your property was priced at 250,000 euros and you sold it by listing it yourself on the MLS system, you would save yourself 6,050 euros on an immediate sale and 5,050 if it sold in 6 months. If your property sales price is half a million euros, then an immediate sale saves you an incredible 12,200 euros and a sale in 6 months saves you an amazing 11,300 euros. Are you starting to get the picture?

Hopefully, these numbers show you just how worthwhile this strategy can be. The other thing I hope that you see is that because the membership fee is so low, this strategy actually pays off more the longer your property is on the market. For example, you can have your property on the market for six months and only lose 1,200 euros from the sales price. This gives you the advantage of being able to try your property at a higher price to see if the market will accept it and if after six months it is clear that the price you want is too high, you can reduce your price drastically to sell and still only pay the other agents 2.5% which when added to your 1,200 euros for six months MLS membership will still be less than listing it with a local agent. In this example, the 1,200 you paid for the MLS system in the first six months can be seen as the price you paid to learn if you could sell at a higher price, and even after all of this, you will still have paid much less than if you had allowed another agent to list the property on your behalf.

So herein lies the benefit of doing your own listing on the MLS system. You can put your property on for any price that you want. So, for example, if you really want to sell your property quickly, you can list it very cheaply (priced to sell) and sell it quickly, or you can put it at the higher end of properties in your area as an experiment for a couple of months and see if other agents have the buyer looking for a property just like yours for whom price is no problem (yes, unlikely but it will only cost you a few hundred euros off of the final sales price to do this for a few months and find out).

Lastly, the 50/50 commission shares with the other agents on the Multiple Listing system is a real estate agent's norm, but it is not law. There is nothing in the legislation to say that you have to offer the other agent 2.5% of the final sales price (or that the estate agent has to charge the seller 5% of the sales price in the first place). You could decide that because you're not in a rush to sell, you can put the property on the system and offer to pay your partner agent (the one who finds the eventual buyer) 1.5% of the sales price, for example, and save yourself 1%. Not every agent will go for this, but depending on your property or their cash flow at the time, some may, and the best thing about the MLS system is that you have to declare the profit share available as part of your property listing, which forms a binding contract. As such, there will be no need for negotiation with these agents; they will simply look at your listing, look at the price and the commission share that they are being offered, and if they are prepared to work for what you are paying, then they will, and if it's too little for them, they won't. No negotiation or argument is required. It is a perfect filtering system to get the agent partners you want at the price you are willing to pay.

So now, not only are you saving the 2.5% that you would have paid to the listing agent, but you can also save 1% (or at least 0. 5%) of the sales price from the agent who finds the buyer. (I told you estate agents were going to hate me for writing this book.)

Different MLS systems have differing rules. Obviously, they were designed to serve real estate agents and work for them, not against them, so you may have to be shrewd when you apply for an account. Luckily not all MLS systems require you to be a limited company to become a member. Becoming a limited company with the setup cost, taxes, and legal accounting requirements will have a big impact on the validity of this strategy, especially for the properties at the lower end of the price scale. The good news is that most of the time, this will not be necessary. Some MLS systems will allow you to join if you are self-employed (aka Autonomo in Spain), which you can arrange at the offices of your local Gestore (Bookkeeper) in about an hour for less than 100 euros. Whether you join as a limited company or a self-employed sole trader, you are not lying or scamming the system. You are actively working in real estate. You are a real estate agency with one client, yourself, and one property on your books to sell, namely yours. Others will not require you to be a business at all, but overall, my advice is that if you find the membership rules of one MLS system prohibitive, try the others. The worst-case scenario will be that your property will be listed by a local agent on the MLS that you can't join and self listed on the ones that you can. It all adds to the increased probability of getting your property sold quickly and for a price you want.

So fancy saving 11,000 euros on the sale of your 500,000 euro villa, or at least 5,050 euros on the sale of our 250,000 euro apartment? Then join up and become a member of your local MLS (or two) and play the odds in exactly the same way your local estate agent was going to play them if you had given him the listing.

Oh, and lastly, but by no means least. Being a member of the MLS has one more extremely powerful benefit. Memberships not only give you access to the other agents but also gives you access to their listings. As such, using it to look at the comparable properties in your area is one of the best ways to know exactly what your property is really worth on the current open market and then price your property appropriately. Regardless of the other options presented in this book, the MLS is, without doubt, the best place to get these up-to-date 'For sale' (not sold) comparables and to see how long overpriced properties sit on the market. This information should help you set the price of your property appropriately, which in all honestly, in terms of saving you time by not overpricing your property, is worth the monthly fees of the MLS alone.

How to game the MLS: Using the multiple listings system to pay less in commission for a better service

Before I get started, let me tell you that real estate agents are going to hate me for telling you this. How to use the multiple listings system to pay less in commission for a better service

Like all advances in technology, because of the advent of Multiple Listing Systems, the whole concept of giving property to an estate agent exclusively is pretty much null and void. I mean, seriously, if you're an estate agent, why would you take a property on your books exclusively and not put it on the Multiple Listing System. Multi listings Systems, or MLS as they are usually called, allow agents to pool the properties they have listed for sale on one database. Therefore once you are a member of an MLS, you have the right to share the properties you have for sale with other agents, and simultaneously you get access to the properties they have listed for sale (yes, yes, I know I have explained this but according to Anthony Robbin's repetition is the mother of skill). The advantages of this are dramatic, and I can assure you have saved the business of many an estate agent over the years simply because it greatly increases the probability of the agent getting a sale. For example, if Agent B, who has his office in Marbella, lists a 3-bed Townhouse in Elvira, although in the most logical area for people looking for a Marbella property, he still might not find the right client to buy it. Enter the Multi listings system upon whence he has uploaded this Marbella townhouse; he is now assisted in selling the property by other agencies up and down the coast or even country, all eager to match their buyer with his property. Let's say, for example's sake, he eventually gets a call from Agent A, an estate agency in Sotogrande, a full hour's drive away. Agent A has been running Spanish Costa property marketing campaigns, and as a result of targeting ABC1 demographics (now known as high net worth's), he not only gets buyers interested in Sotogrande but a few who are looking for property in Marbella as well. He now no longer needs to go looking for property in Marbella himself to satisfy their needs. He does not even need to call a few choice friends in agencies he has met over the years to ask them if they have anything suitable. He simply goes to the MLS system for which he is a member and looks up the areas in Marbella his new clients are most interested in and then filters this search by their property preference, i.e., a three-bedroom townhouse with a garden and voila, up pops agent B's listing ready with all the details for him to send it to the client, arrange a viewing and if sold, be guaranteed half of the sales commission.

In all honesty, it is a great system, and 99% of the time works flawlessly, which in itself is an amazing feat knowing the cutthroat arena of real estate, and in understanding how the system works, it is clear to see that there really is no benefit for an estate agent to not put your property on the MLS system, I mean what would they gain? Yes, if they sell your property without it, they make all of the commission for themselves, but in order to do this, they take the risk of removing the greatest tool and asset they have available for getting it sold in the first place.

Truth be told, an estate agent will only keep a no-brainer of a property off the MLS books. If they list a 1500 m2 two-story villa with underbuild of 2000m^2 with a manicured garden plot and solarium, all mod cons, and a private pool for the same price as a two-bedroom apartment in the same area, then yes, they will keep this off the books because it's an absolute slam dunk that they will make this sale, but even then some will still list this property hedging their bets between the extra time it takes them to sell it without the help of the other agents on the MLS and the 2.5% that they will lose by putting it on the system and having a reservation on it tomorrow.

So in Shakespearean terms (to use the MLS or not to use the MLS, that is the question), in most cases, the risk of not using it far outweighs the benefit. Another reason for this other than the obviously improved ease of finding a buyer is that even though you, the seller, were sure that the listing agent you chose from the 5 or 6 available real estate agents in your area was the right one for you and the right person to sell it, you are only going to give them a certain amount of time to get the job done before you are forced to start thinking about offering it to someone else. And if that new agent doesn't work out and they can't sell the thing, you will move it to another agent until you find the agent who can get it sold.

This puts real estate agents in a position of choice. They can either greatly increase their chances of selling your property by putting it on an MLS and selling it with the aid of another estate agent, and although getting only half of the commission, at least make some money and have a happy, satisfied client ready to give those all-important testimonials and referrals, or they can hold onto your property tightly with the hope that their passing trade or marketing campaigns bring them in a buyer who wants just what you have to offer and they can make the full sale commission. The probability of the latter is fully less than half of the former, and yet, believe it or not, some estate agents still do take this risk, risking the success of your sale and peace of mind to get a higher commission.

From a business, perspective is quite simply nonsense. In addition to that, if they are part of the Multiple Listing System, they are paying for it anyway, so it really doesn't hurt them at all to put the property on it and show it to anybody who the other agents on the system can bring forward, whilst they are still trying to sell it themselves. If they can sell it themselves, then they are still in the position to earn 100% of the Commission for the sale, and it hasn't cost them a penny more as they were paying for the Multiple Listing System to gain access to the properties of other agents anyway. And considering being a member is not hard; uploading your property to the MLS takes maybe 20 minutes worth of work and potentially the odd few minutes to make updates on the system on their computer.

So what does all of this mean for you? Well, back in the day (and I really am showing my age now), because agents wanted properties exclusively, the competition between agents in the same area (and often on the same street) meant that they would offer you a lower commission for the right to sell yours, especially if they thought it was a good deal and they would be able to sell it quickly.

Back then, it made much more sense for estate agents to have the exclusive right to sell a property, knowing that they had no competition in terms of getting the thing sold. They knew that the time and effort which they spent on it, the time they spent in learning it back to front, building the marketing plan, and doing the actual marketing was not going to be in vain because they had no competition until it was either sold or taken away from them due to their inability to sell it.

If you listed the property with them on a non-exclusive contract, then they would have to go through the same listing, learning, and marketing efforts just knowing that other agents who had the exact same property for sale could sell it right from under their feet, making all of the cost and efforts in preparing your property for sale a waste. This is why some estate agents will charge you a higher commission for a non exclusive contract, but trust me in terms of its benefits to you its worth it.

Nowadays, this kind of exclusivity rarely exists. If it exists at all, it is usually with regards to new build properties where exclusivity is given for a certain number of units on a development. But for one single resale property, it is far less likely because it doesn't make economic sense, and this is a fact that you can use to your advantage because when you choose the real estate agent to list your property with, you can still use the fact that you're giving them the opportunity to earn 100% of the commission if they can. This means that you can negotiate commission with them and if your property seems attractive to them and appears to be something which they can sell on their own and quickly, they will consider it.

Why would they consider a reduction in commission?

Okay, so unless you've taken my previous advice of putting the property on the Multi Listing System yourself, if you take your property to a real estate agent (as I have pointed out before), the fact that he's the person who put the listing up means that he has the opportunity to earn 100% of the commission from the sale if he can indeed sell the property by himself. He can alternatively sell it with the aid of another estate agent and get 50% of the Commission.

Most agents will tell you that they are bound by a 5% commission rate because they will have to split this with another agent 50/50. This is true; most sharing agents will not want to bring their buyers to see other agents' listings for less than a 2.5% share of the commission. So if the standard commission rate is for a shared sale is 2.5% each, how could he offer to sell your property for less? How could he offer to sell it, for example, a 4% commission? If he knows, he may have to split half of that with another agent who will be expecting his full 2.5%. Well, the truth of the matter is, his duty to the other agents is none of your business. If he thinks that he can sell the property himself and wants to take the kind of risk that we took back in the days before the Multiple Listing System existed, then he can agree to take the property on and be the one to list it for you with an agreed commission of 4%. This gives him the opportunity to make 100% of this 4% commission which no other agent has, if he can sell the property without any assistance from others. Remember the person who lists the property directly, i.e., the person who you sign a contract with has the opportunity to sell the property without aid from others and receive 100% of the commission (that would be 4% in this case), whereas any agent who brings the buyer to a listing on the MLS system has the maximum potential to earn only half of a normal commission (normal commissions being 5%) which under normal circumstances would be a maximum of 2.5% of the commission if the buyer he brings to the property buys it). Look, Ma, I'm doing maths!!!

If, by the way, you actually care about what happens to your listing agent (which would be rather unusual and very, very impractical), hopefully, this will give you peace of mind. The estate agent actually has two options. He can either go ahead and upload your property to the Multiple Listing System and say,

'This property for sale is available for the usually shared commission based on a 50/50 split, but please be aware that the full commission on this property is only 4%, so your share of the commission upon sale will be 2%.

If he is smart enough to do this, then he gains the best of both worlds because he has the opportunity to sell your property exclusively and to earn 100% of the commission if he can sell it alone (because you gave him the listing), but loses nothing if he can't because he still only pays half of the commission that you pay him to the third party if it's sold with another agent. For the listing agent, this is his best-case scenario and what a smart realtor would do, and it's definitely what I would do.

Alternatively, if the other agents are not interested in selling the property at a reduced commission, he always has the option to cut his losses and accept the fact that since he was the listing agent, he took the opportunity (or the risk depending on how you see it), because he believed that he could sell the property alone and so agreed a reduced 4% commission with you. So if he gets to the point where he realises that he, in fact, cannot sell it on his own and has to upload it to the MLS system to seek the help of selling it with another agent; for example, if he has had it on his books for four months of your six-month contract with no viewings and you the seller are clearly unhappy about it and about to take it from him and list it with another agent, he can cut his losses and accept the help of another agent from the MLS system, pay this agent his expected 2.5% and suffer the loss of a lower commission to himself of 1.5% for having taken a risk based on the fact that he thought he could sell it unaided and failed.

Not every agent will do this (most real estate agents are not really forward-thinking in terms of business and strategy), but if he's a sensible businessman and takes the view that every single business decision comes with risks, then this strategy will work. He will understand and accept the fact that the risk he took was that he thought he could sell the property on his own and earn all of the commission. As such, he backed himself (or gambled depending on how you see it) and asked for the position of exclusivity in his arrangement with you to be the only one listing the property and as such, the one with the right to share the sale and commission or keep it to himself. That gave him the chance to have no other competition in the sale, and if having no other competition in the sale of your property, he failed to sell it, if he was misguided in his belief that he could sell it on his own and earn all of the commission, if after a period of time he realised that it made more sense to sell it through another agent and make some money rather than lose it altogether and make no money, then that was simply his business decision, his risk, and his responsibility. Don't worry about him too much; if he managed to sell it with the help of another agent before his lack of performance lost him the listing completely, at least he got something back and will have learned a valuable business lesson in the process whilst still making more money from the transaction than if he just had just given up and walked away from it.

The risk of this strategy to you is that if he does not have the ability, marketing, or skill to sell your property without another agent yet is stubborn and won't share it, or if the other agents on the MLS won't show your property to their clients for a lower commission demanding the standard 2.5%, and he won't accept his self-inflicted loss and settle for a reduction on his half, then your property will miss opportunities to be sold, and unfortunately for you, you will be none the wiser. You won't know how many other agents contacted him with potential clients who wanted to buy it and would have been happy to clinch the sale if they could keep their expected commission to 2.5%. You won't know how many MLS agents sent out requests for properties matching your exact description, which he ignored, confident in the belief that he did not need their help and would be able to sell the property himself and earn all of that lovely extra money. But that said, all of this downside exists even if you agree to pay him the standard 5% commission or even if you pay him 7%, so there really is not much to lose by trying to negotiate to pay him less.

So ask your listing agent if he is part of an MLS system. If he says yes, then tell him that as such, you are aware that as the listing agent, he has the potential to earn the most from your listing, and as such, you want a reduction on the agreed commission from the standard rate. If he says no, then thank him for his time and go to the agent next door. In a competitive business world, someone will take the deal.

So, in summary, the MLS system puts you in a very good position to bargain and reduce the commission you pay on the sale of your property, but the effectiveness of this strategy to meet your primary goal really depends on if the real estate agent you are dealing with is the kind of business owner who has a common-sense approach to risk and reward, understands about cutting his losses (wipe his mouth and move on as we say in the property game) or is the type who will want to dig his heels in until the end of your contract, to try to sell it for maximum commission but ultimately wasting your time and costing you sales.

Remember that as the seller of a property, you are a business too, and you will have to carefully select your listing agent to make sure that his business outlook matches your needs. The good news is that after a period of time, you will fall perfectly within your rights to remove the listing from him.

You simply say

'Well, I gave this listing to you. You didn't sell it yourself or sell it in conjunction with anybody else, so now I'm removing it from you and giving it to the agency next door.'

The Multiple Listing System is a very powerful tool not just for estate agents but for the sellers if they understand it and know how to use it as leverage. If you as a seller understand its potential effect on the decisions of sensible business people (please pay attention to this statement. Only sensible business people and agencies which operate as a business will see the value in this type of approach), then it can lead to you selling your home and paying less in the bargain.

A word of caution. The world is full of stubborn people and full of stubborn people who run businesses yet can't see beyond the end of their nose (business people who know nothing about negotiation, or about playing the odds, risk, rewards, or any of these other very basic business concepts). So when presented with this opportunity, these types of business owners either turn you down flat or accept the challenge in the hope of the spoils but renege on the common sense option to sell with help when confronted with the potential losses.

Luckily for you, this is not a great problem. There are five more estate agents on your road and maybe ten more in your area. For this to work, you only need one open-minded and a diligently good one. And the funny thing is, all of the agents who pass on your offer will still have the opportunity to sell your property once it hits the Multi Listings System, so even if they find your perfect buyer through their marketing, you won't miss out, they will be the ones who missed out on earning full commission because I guarantee to you, that as a third party listing found on the MLS if they have a buyer who fits your property, they will introduce that client to the agency you eventually listed your property with and take the money for the shared sale.

So there you have it, estate agents are going to hate me for this, but I have just taught you how to game the Multi Listings System (what hip kids call to finesse the system) as a seller to get the best of both worlds for yourself.

All you need is one agency; whether they're more open-minded, more attuned to think outside the box, better business people, or desperately in need of the business and the money, their motivation does not matter. All you need is one agency that will accept your offer to pay the lower commission of 4% (or even 3.5%, but I would not take the Mickey and offer any less than this unless the sales price is north of 500,000 euros) for the exclusive right to list and the opportunity to earn more by performing better. They are taking a risk to earn more by betting on themselves rather than betting on the probability of the crowd. This is the essence of business, and somewhere in your circle of real estate agents, there will be a business owner who knows this, understands this, and is willing to play the game.

Top Tips for working with Estate Agents

- Get the estate agent
- Use ethical bribery to get the estate agent to notice you
- Use ethical bribery to get the estate agent to prioritize your sale
- Use old school ethical financial bribery to get the estate agent to prioritize your sale

- Use the MLS system as a bargaining tool with your estate agent

- Use the MLS system as your number one tool when selling FSBO

CHAPTER 8: VIEWING YOUR HOME

Don't crowd the estate agents viewing

So we have by now seen that there are two distinct and separate strains to our strategy. The first is to take personal responsibility for the sale of our home and proactively take all measures that are in our control to get it sold. The second is to take our time to find an estate agent who we trust and then to strike an agreement with them that suits our needs and to work with them in getting a deal done.

With regards to the second, it is important now that we have taken the time to find an agent (and beat him into the submission of taking a lower commission on our sale), that we trust him enough to work without obstructing him, and one of the ways we can avoid obstructing him is to try to ensure that we are out of the property when he is bringing a potential buyer to view.

Don't be home when your estate agent is showing your property to buyers. This might sound like a contradiction to some of the earlier points, but it's really just a reiteration of the fact that you need to spend some time to find a good estate agent who you really trust, and also put them on a probation period, not to sell your house but just to see how they perform. If after this period they are not performing in a way that you want them to, cancel that contract and move on to another. Once you're confident that you've got the right estate agent showing your home, you have to give them the trust to do their job.

I have to be honest with you, I would personally like to at least meet the buyers too if it's at all possible, but in reality, there is no doubt about it. If somebody is walking around the house with the owner there, whether silent as a mouse or interjecting into the conversation all the time, then the whole process is going to feel as if they are intruding as opposed to viewing a home. They won't have the comfortability to make the comments that they want to make, ask the questions they want to ask, some of which will be buying questions, and lead your agent to a sale.

This is one of the powers of our two-pronged approach. All of the leads, viewings and potential buyers which you generate from your own activity are yours to tour so you can show them your home the way you see fit. So now that you have your own potential buyers that you can tour your home in your own way, there is no need to interfere with the estate agent's buyers and the way the estate agent shows your property.

So, there is a lot to be said for being present, but only at the viewings, you arrange. Obviously, the best option would be if you were not living in the house at all. This is why we strongly advise only to market your rental property when it is vacant and not when it has a tenant in it (regardless of if they are a short-term or long-term tenant). It is so much easier to sell even a holiday rental property when it is empty, and trust me, I know;

I have taken many an investor to apartments with wives rapidly throwing clothes in cupboards or even worst, half-naked tourists sat sweating on the sun terrace, having been interrupted by us from their Strawberry Daiquiris. Yes, it shows that the property is rentable, but other than that, trust me, it's not a good look.

But unfortunately, circumstances may dictate that you have no choice in the matter, so if you are selling the house in which you reside, then make sure that whenever your house is being shown by your estate agent, you go out for a drink. Go have a coffee and come back when the viewings are over; it won't be too inconvenient because this will only be when an estate agent is showing your property. Obviously, when you are showing your own property, it will be completely different, and you will have to be the person who must be open enough to listen to those hurtful comments, answer those difficult questions and respond to them in a way that is positive for the buyer. Respond to them in a way that is not defensive or protective but honest and enthusiastic about the good stuff that outweighs the bad, but don't worry about this too much now; we will get to how to do this in our sections on sales and negotiation.

But when it is your real estate agent showing your property, just get out of the house. If for any reason you cannot leave the premises, then restrict your participation to greeting the estate agent and the potential buyers as they arrive, tell them that you will be at their disposal if they need you or have any questions, and then get the hell out of there. Do not under any circumstances follow them around the house because as small and friendly as you are, you will intimidate them and take away from them the experience of looking at your home objectively, finding out for themselves that that is the perfect property for them and making an offer on it.

You might think that it is a good thing to be there so that you can answer any questions straight away, to have that discussion, clarify those points and build that rapport but ask any estate agent, and nothing could be further from the truth. If you follow them around the house and intimidate them, there's absolutely every single chance; they will think that although your property has everything that they wanted, somehow your property was still not right for them because, for some strange reason (namely you), they didn't feel comfortable in it. How many things have you bought that made you feel uncomfortable? (skinny jeans and corsets bought by fashion victims excluded) not many, I would guess. Well, then you need to make sure that you do not make potential buyers uncomfortable in your home.

They need to feel comfortable while they're viewing it. They need to walk away from your home with a feeling of comfortability, that warm glow that you get when you can see yourself enjoying something. Standing behind them as they look at the damp on the wall in your third bedroom is not going to allow them to have that. So just don't be there. That's it.

Greet them and then retire to the part of the house where like the children of old, you are neither seen nor heard unless summoned. If you have a shed, this is a great time to do your pottering; estate agent viewing is a perfect time to do some light gardening or read a magazine in the conservatory. It is definitely not the time to sit sprawled across the sofa in the living room watching Formula 1 at 100 decibels to get the feeling of being trackside or catching up on the Coronation Street omnibus, looking up every time they nod at you and shyly and walk through your living room to another part of the house embarrassed at their intrusion into your home and the interruption to your life that they are causing.

Well, isn't this correct, you may ask? If they are the 15th person to view your home and they insist on coming at 7 pm in the evening, are they not intruding on my life? If you think that this is correct and they are, then please allow me to give you a slight shift of perspective. When you are selling your home, unless you are the person showing it, if you are in it when it is being shown, they are not intruding on you; you are intruding on them.

So whilst you have retired to the conservatory to allow them to have a good look around the house, if any questions do arise and are brought to you by the agent, you will be in the perfect position of fortunately still being available to answer them, and they will appreciate you taking the time from what you are busy doing to assist them as opposed to feeling that their presence is an inconvenience to you. As you now have a written house selling plan which allows you to know your property inside out, back to front, warts and all, you will have the answers to their questions, including all the rebuttals to potential objections.

So, in summary, the best-case scenario is an empty property, staged like a show home and shown by the estate agent to his potential buyers. If you live in the property that you are selling, then try to arrange viewings for times that it is convenient for you to leave them to view and come back once they have finished. If you cannot leave, then make yourself scarce, find the place in the house where you will be of least interruption to them. Retire to the least important part of your home so that you are not sat slap bang in the middle of the living room as they walk in and out. Go to the smallest bedroom because potential buyers will not tend to spend a lot of time looking at the bonus room, whereas if you sit on the terrace, you will take away the ability for the buyer to sit on the terrace themselves, taking in the view and dreaming what it would be like to own this apartment and do this for themselves someday.

Overall let the real estate agent who you've taken the time to research and employ do her job, trust in her ability and her desire to sell your house in the process secure in the knowledge that if they don't, you have one hell of a plan B.

Viewing Times

Allow me to make a quick note of the timing of your open house or general property viewings.

Houses sell when people see as much natural light as possible. Natural light just seems to enhance and glorify homes. So you want to make sure that you organise your viewings for the best times of the day to show off the best qualities of your home.

If you have a balcony that catches the sun in the morning but not in the afternoon, depending on which aspect you want to show to the buyer, arrange viewing times accordingly to either appeal to a sun worshipper or the buyer interested in ensuring that they have sufficient shade. If the best quality of your house is the way that it catches the sun so beautifully in the morning, then arrange viewings in the morning. If you think that the best quality is that it has a killer view over the pool as early evening draws, then make sure you arrange your viewings starting from the late afternoon.

This is obviously going to be harder with viewings than with open houses. With an open house, you dictate the time autocratically, leaving people to fit it into their schedule and either turn up or not. Property viewings are a much more democratic affair where two or sometimes even three people have to synchronise their diaries in order to find a time which suits all, meaning that in terms of getting the viewing at the time you want, you've got more organisation to do. So if, for example, they can only do Tuesday afternoon, but it's essential for them to see that glorious morning sun warm the 'Mudruga' (morning dew) from your terrace, then see if you can put the viewing back one day. Do it in the morning on Wednesday. It might seem like a lot of work, but as they say, you only get one chance to make a first impression so take the time and effort to put your property's best foot forwards.

If you're doing an open house, you need to make sure that the times you are open are specifically designed to highlight the best aspects of your property. If you have a garden in which the flowers bloom at a certain time of the day, make sure to open your house to prospective buyers between the times that those flowers are blooming, standing upright, and looking at the most potent and beautiful, then make a visit to your garden the starting and ending point of your house tour.

If you have a neighbourhood with noisy dogs, but they have a routine, and you know that they will be out for their daily walk at a certain time of the day. Make sure that you organise your open house based on the times that those dogs out. Or even better, if you get on with your neighbour (as difficult as it might be, you know, because of their noisy dogs and all), ask them to take the dogs out for the time of the day that your open house or viewing has been organized or at the very least give them something from the butchers to chew on, thereby throwing both the dogs and you a bone (real estate agent speaks for giving someone a chance just in case the pun was lost on you).

In terms of putting your best foot forward, try to include as many things as you can; your house selling plan and final walk-through will help you with this immensely. Once you have identified the key selling points or your home, you will know the best times instinctively to show it leaving you to only try to negotiate for all of your viewings or open houses to occur at these times.

Now when I talk about showing your property in terms of putting your best foot forward and allowing people to see the best version of your home, this might be seen as disingenuous. Personally, I just compare it to a first date. Most people wouldn't go to a first date (or a job interview, for that matter), belch, scratch themselves in intimate places, cough loudly, dress badly, pick their noses or talk in a vulgar manner. Most people would do everything in their power to show the best sides of themselves; first, the logic being that once people see all the great stuff that you have to offer, they will be happy to accept the negative stuff we all do that comes along with it (yes you too you belching, scratching, nose picking dressed like a badly wrapped Xmas present hypocrite). I mean, everyone has negative traits, so they won't be that surprised when they finally discover your annoying habits because everybody has them. But you want to give yourself a chance by showing them all the great stuff that comes along with the fact that you snore or floss in the living room first, right. In fact, in human psychology, you will find that most people see and pay attention to negative things first (you have two thousand years of human evolution which formed our Amygdala to seek out danger as a pre-coded element of survival of the species enacting our fight or flight response to thank for that). So presenting only your positive traits is, in fact, simply balancing the tables. Humans need no help in finding what's wrong with something as a part of their self-preservation programming, so the act of showing what's right with it is essential if you want to have a fighting chance in getting its approval and in both job search and dating this is standard behaviour which most people consider appropriate, so why would you approach to selling your property be any different? It is up to you to show and highlight all of the benefits of your property before they themselves find out the downsides because they'll already be looking for all the things that are or could go wrong with it. Showing it in the best light, its best position on a nice day is not disingenuous; it's just allowing them to see everything that's right with it, which is your job, as opposed to everything that's wrong with it, which is not only their job but their natural evolutionary instinct.

No People, No Little People, No Pets

As part of the house viewing, I also hope that it is, needless to say, get your pets out of your house. It should come as no surprise when I tell you that you need to clear all mammals out of your home, all of them, starting with your pets. You may know that Fido is a big soppy Great Dane and loves nothing more than to be stroked by people, but this is still a big no no. Even if your potential buyer is a dog lover, petting your dog isn't always the best scenario for your potential buyer and will be a distraction to the points that you are trying to make when selling your home, but if Winston (as in Ray Winston, not Churchill), the bulldog you know is as the big softy who loves people, runs up to greet a potential buyer who is absolutely petrified of dogs, take my word for it, even if your property is their personal Shangri la, you have probably just lost a sale. So get them out of there; it's just common sense.

When the buyers are looking at your home, you want them to come and pay attention to your home, not your Dog, pet Rabbit, pet Iguana, domesticated Tiger (if you are Mike Tyson selling a mansion to avoid going broke or Joey Exotic doing the same) unless these animals are included in the particulars of the sale. And yes, before you ask, the same goes for cats; they got a cat flap, so get him out of there.

Also, as the very famous advert goes, if you have pets, you've probably gone nose blind, which means that you are now immune to the smell of your pets and the smells which they create (smokers, please take note as this also applies to your pet cigarettes). Unfortunately, your potential buyers will not be, so you're going to have to spend extra time cleaning, air freshening, opening doors and windows, and making sure (if at all possible) that you get those smells out.

As I said, if you are a smoker, exactly the same thing goes. Yes, I totally understand that you're sick of the government telling you all the places that you can't smoke, meaning that the one place you can at least smoke is your home. Well, sorry to tell you, mate, but not anymore. Sure, you can smoke in your home, but as an ex-smoker, I can assure you that the smell of your smoke is getting into your curtains, on your walls, and into every pore of your house. That's what smoke does; you are going to need to freshen up your whole home if you want to get rid of that smoke and sell it to a non-smoker. In fact, you are going to have to freshen up your home even if you're selling your home to other smokers because even as a smoker, I wouldn't have bought a house that reeked of nicotine. Hypocritical, yes, but this will still be the case for most smokers looking for property. When you are buying something, you want it to be presented in the best possible light, not how you expect it to be three years after you have been using it. That is why so many people love the smell of a new car; nobody queues up to buy a car that smells of kid's vomit, summer sweat, and late-night pizza, even though this is how your car may well smell two years after you bought it.

So we have cleared our home of Dogs and Cats; in fact, just include any other mammals or animals you have in this list (Michael Jackson fans get that chimpanzee out of here too). Whatever it is, no matter how much you love it, yes, I know it's part of the family but save that for the Xmas Jumper photo, get it out of there.

Ok, what else? Well, this may upset you, but those other mammals that you love so dearly, unfortunately, are probably not going to help you to sell your home either. Yes, I'm talking about your kids. Your children might also be a good idea to get out of the house too. No disrespect to your children, I know that they're beautiful and funny and polite, but to some of your potential buyers they can be as terrifying as Winston the Bulldog (to parents and non-parents alike). Plus, if you have been in the game as long as I have, that bored look in the eyes of your teen daughter when we interrupt her homework to take a peek at her room tells me volumes regarding how many viewings you have had, how long you have had the property on the market and how desperate you are to sell.

So it is true that somebody looking to start a new family might be absolutely bowled over by your adorable little children in your home. The problem is you probably haven't trained your children to sell your home. So with the absence of this high-level 'million-dollar listing' training, they will simply do what children do, which might well be distracting. Even worse, they may well point out flaws of house by accident. Your potential buyer will have more than enough opportunity to see that your house is perfect for children just by walking around it and seeing the well-appointed nursery or the neat and tidy kids room with all of the neatly packed away toys or the teenager's posters on the wall and guitar in the corner. Whatever is already there will show them just how comforting and homely

183

your property is. They will be able to look around these spaces whilst listening to you happily tell them which room is for which child and why they prefer it. This is preferable to the many times that I have taken potential buyers to apartments complete with a sulky teenager sat at their desk who, unlike you, the parent, finds it much harder to hide the fact that they are sick of all these viewings and people disturbing them, coming into their room and gawking at them like a zoo animal. I mean, let's face it, your snarky teenager doesn't even like it when you come into their room, and you own the goddamn house. So if it's possible to arrange the viewings for times when they are not there, maybe when they are out at Martial Arts practice, band practice, or a friend's house doing a school project (teenage code for snogging their secret partner or smoking a bong), or even just hanging out, it would be much better. Equally, when the younger kids have gone down to the park for a couple of hours or over to a friend's house for a play date, this is the time that you want to try to organise your back-to-back viewings. This will allow you to get the full benefit of showing all aspects of your home to prospective buyers a well as doubling down on allowing them to see other people are interested in the property (the trick which we mentioned earlier in this book), and also give you the benefit of arranging your family life around the viewings so that you minimize the negativity and disruption that they can cause.

Top Tips when potential buyers are viewing your home

- Be out of the house if the estate agent has organized the viewing

- If you can not leave the house be out of the way

- No Children, no Pets, or other distractions

- If you have pets or are a smoker make an extra effort to neutralize the smells created

- If you are conducting the viewing spend extra time with the potential buyer at the end to build rapport

CHAPTER 9: SALES TECHNIQUES & NEGOTIATIONS

NEGOTIATION

WIN

WIN

Salesmanship

Using our two-pronged approach, you will now be running a parallel sales structure for your property to that of your real estate agent. You are running our own advertisements leading to getting our own inquiries and ultimately leading to your own viewings. So obviously (as none of this is done through the help of your estate agent), with regards to these inquiries, you are the person in control. You are now in control of not only showing them your property as the property tour guide, but of the sales to get them interested in buying it and the negotiation process required to come to an agreement and get it sold.

This is super important and will require some of your focus and attention because you may never have made any form of sales before at any time in your life, but now you are making sales, and more importantly, unlike the person trying to sell a cheese grater for 1.99 outside of a supermarket, you are doing the hardest type of sales known to man; you are making high-end sales. There are very few things more high-end than property. Property is even more high-end in terms of sales than jewellery, cars, or yachts; in fact, the only thing more high-end than property is more expensive property.

This doesn't mean that you have to become a master salesman to sell your property, but you will have to have some respect for the difficulty of what it is you're trying to achieve, and you definitely will have to put some effort into it if you want to achieve some success, which for you means the sale of your property.

I am not going to recommend that you take a sales course nor teach one here, but I am going to recommend that you take a sales course in the sale of your own property. You are going to need to learn your property not as the home you have lived in or the rental property that you invested in, but as a product that you are marketing and selling to a customer. This change in perspective can be all the difference in seeing your property the way you need to see it to get it sold.

So, in addition to the walkthrough, you need to know your property like the back of your hand. The blueprint or home selling plan that we had you prepare at the beginning of this book will help you to do this.

You are going to use the blueprint to assess your home from the perspective of the buyer, which is something that you probably haven't really done before, even if you think you have. We are going to look at the pros and cons of your property from a commercial perspective, through a completely objective lens which is why although you think that you have thought your property thoroughly, you have probably not.

You have probably not thought about the pros and, more particularly, the cons of your property through the lens of a product you are trying to sell, not because you don't know that these parts of your property exist, but because you are used to them so won't see them the way someone you are asking to part with their hard-earned cash will see them. How logical or illogical they are, how useful or annoying they are, how beneficial or detrimental they are. You probably haven't done this since you yourself bought the property, so now is your time to do it again, looking at your property through the lens of the buyer in order to see it clearly enough to be able to sell it.

Now that you have used your home selling plan to be clear about every negative aspect and weak spot of your property, it is time to prepare your answers to the criticisms, negative remarks and obstacles to selling your property that comes from them when people come to look at your house. If you know something is not in a logical place, as I said before, have your answer to the comment ready before they even say it, but do not point it out (I will explain why a bit later in this chapter).

Explain all of the negative aspects of your home in terms of lower price or potential. For example, if they say that the 2nd bedroom would be better as an en suite, well, having done your appraisal of your property through the lens of a product, you already know this. All thoughts of it being cute and useful to you because your children needed to share it are gone, and you finally face the truth that the bathroom is illogically placed in terms of usefulness and utilization of space. So what do you do? You can explain this away in terms of price;

188

'Yes, that is the way that these apartments were designed, but if you want to, it can be changed. We decided not to do it as it suited our children, but that is one of the reasons the house is priced a bit less than the others on our block.'

Or in terms of potential…

'Yes, it isn't ideal; it worked for us as a family but didn't suit a few of our neighbours, so they had it converted into a 2nd en suite just as you are suggesting. It's easy enough to do, and as well as its increased convenience to you, it will definitely add a lot of value to the house once it's finished.

Or finally, a mixture of both,

'Yes, that's the way they were built, others have done as you suggested, which is easy to do and definitely adds value to your home, we decided not to do it because it suited our family as it was, but we understand that isn't the same for everyone which is why we reduced our selling price to reflect the fact that you might want to do it.'

Many salesmen prefer to try to obscure a product's problems and flaws; this is an approach that I do not condone. I absolutely advocate for showing your best side and explaining the silver lining to the cons of your property, but in terms of obscuring flaws, my personal rule of thumb is; if it seems dishonest or feels like you are lying, then don't do it.

We have already discussed that it is acceptable to present ourselves in the best light, but no, I'm not suggesting you hide the fact that your house has subsidence (although that is really for the valuer to expose). There's nothing wrong with you putting your best foot forward and showing the best potential of your home, and there is definitely nothing wrong with not highlighting its worst points.

'Hi, yes, I am pretty lazy really; I play the lottery every week just praying to never have to work again; I got sacked from one job for misconduct, that's why you see a gap in my CV, but I lied and said I was travelling. Anyway, I'm only here because I really need the money, but as soon as I get a chance, I'm going to leave and try to get a job in travel.'

This is not how you would advise your friend to present themselves at their next job interview, even if it was all true? So do not do a version of this when showing your property. I've known sellers who thought that just by demonstrating the honesty of highlighting the worst aspects of their home, they would win points to the buyer. This rarely works. Often they just point out something to a buyer that the buyer hadn't even realised and given the buyer a reason not to buy or at least why the house is not as attractive as they had previously thought it was.

What you want to be able to do with this information is have a rebuttal to anything that the buyer points out to you. You have to already know it's there and definitely know what you are going to say about it. Have a true and reasonable explanation as to why this issue does not devalue your home.

Also, when touring the house yourself, you need an area to talk to the buyer after the viewing is done. You will want to make the environment cosy so make sure you have somewhere that you can sit your buyer down and talk about what they have seen before they leave.

Estate agents will do this, but they will have to wait until they get back to their office, by which time the charm and comfort of any particular home will have been lost. This gives you a massive opportunity over estate agents. Your estate agent will probably have five or six viewings booked in that morning. So there will be a level of rushing your potential buyers in and out of your home, and if you follow the advice of this book, you will not even be present for any of these hurried viewings.

Due to his schedule, the estate agent only really gets to talk to the buyer about what he has seen on coffee or lunch breaks. His plan will be to get them back to the office at the end of the day to discuss the different properties, but some clients will refuse, so he may never get the opportunity you have to sit the buyer down in your property and discuss their thoughts on it. This is also a gold mine of information for you because if you build rapport and listen to them carefully, they will tell you everything you need to improve for the next viewing. So, have some biscuits or cake available. Have some drinks, Tea, coffee or a soft drink. Show them your home, and then invite them to sit down for a few minutes before they leave. Talk to them; ask them questions such as how long have you been looking? How soon do you want to buy? What are you really looking for? What are your deal breakers? Are you buying with cash, or do you need Finance? Is this the particular area you want in terms of your first choice to buy in, or are you still open area wise? What's the most important thing you want from the property you buy?

Get to know a little bit more about them. This will firstly build rapport between you, and every salesman knows that rapport is probably the key component to any sale, more so than price, benefits or the features of any product. I've known lots of people buy a property or make a choice between two competing properties because they like the seller so much. So don't just find out about them, tell them about you; tell them about how long you've owned a house, tell them about your lovely neighbours, tell them about your children growing up in the home or what you did with the rental returns from the

191

investment, tell them the funny story about that one-holiday rental you had, tell them that your children have now left home and as 'empty nesters' you need to downsize, tell them about how much you'd love to stay if you could afford to. Tell them that what you want to see is for the house to go to another good family who could have the kind of experiences in it that you had. Tell them these things and build that rapport over a nice drink and a plate of biscuits. Remember, facts tell, stories sell. This isn't going to sell your house every single time, but it is going to put your property way ahead of all the other people's properties whom they have been rushed through by estate agents. It will make the experience of visiting your property more memorable which is great because people are more likely to revisit the ones they remember the most; it will give the potential buyer a good feeling when they remember visiting your property which is a powerful tool as people buy based on emotions and you will be attaching emotion to your viewing whereas most other viewings will have none.

The two-pronged approach gives you the opportunity to benefit from all of the things that your estate agent will do for you and the benefit of doing for yourself all of the things that she won't. Take this opportunity and be more personable when you tour the property yourself, be the opposite of the estate agent in a rush, build that rapport and greatly increase your chances of getting a sale.

Hot Buttons and the Money Shot

There are two key tools that you can leverage in the sale of every single house; they are hot buttons and the money shot.

The money shot is the number one most sellable feature of your property. This is the number one thing that makes your property more desirable, more unique, and more of a must-have; it's the thing that puts your property over and above all others.

The second tool in selling your home is finding out the most important specific aspects of a property that your buyer really wants. In sales, we call this their 'Hot button.' Every single buyer has one thing that they cherish or hold in importance over and above absolutely everything else. This is to say that, if when taking all of the competing considerations into account, location, price, orientation, age, design, proximity to amenities, pool, garden size and terrace if they had to choose just one thing that was the most important to them in deciding if this is the property they want to buy or not, that one most important thing would be their hot button.

In sales, our aim is to question the buyer and pay close attention to what they say with the aim of finding their hot button. Once you have found it, you are much closer to closing the sale than with any other aspect of the whole process. We call it a hot button as opposed to 'the primary influence' or 'the must have' for a reason, we call it a button because once pressed, it motivates the buyer to say yes to the purchase, so once you find it, you press it, you press it a lot. By pressing it, I mean that you remind them that however many other aspects of the property are less than perfect for them, with regards to this one overwhelming thing, this most important aspect of their purchase, your property is perfect. This is how you press their hot button by finding out what is most important to them in buying a property and then showing them how your property matched that essential need. Once you can press their button by doing this, you press and then press it again. Some salesmen press it so many times that they could be sued for harassment, but I do not advise this. Subtlety is the key, be subtle but make sure that you push that button. (Why do I hear a Pussycat dolls song playing vaguely in the background of my mind whilst I write this paragraph, strange?)

Ok, so let's start with an example of the first tool, the money shot. I have a very good friend and investor who renovated his villa. He knew that although his villa had a fantastic location, and his renovation works were so extensive that they were just shy of flattening the place and rebuilding it from the ground up, most of his efforts were going to be missed as 'features' and as in all sales, the deciding factor was going to be something emotive as opposed to practical.

But he filled the house with features nonetheless. He converted the five bedrooms to seven bedrooms. He put in underfloor heating, renovated two bathrooms, cut back the trees, rewired the whole house, reorganized the air conditioning and separated the heating creating a backup system, landscaped the gardens and built an outside bar and snack area so that you could hang out by the pool all day. It truly was a magnificent renovation, and once completed, his property looked like a new building as opposed to the 30 plus-year-old property that it was.

But before he had done any of this work when he was still in the planning stage, we viewed the property together, and both agreed that the sea view from the upstairs bedroom and terrace was absolutely astounding. It was a uniquely clear view out to Morocco, which was as picturesque as it was stunning. This, without a doubt, was the money shot.

So being a very, very experienced developer, when he renovated the property, he expanded on this aspect and made sure that the upstairs sea view was now visible, not just from the master bedroom and terrace, but also from the master bedroom itself, two of the other bedrooms, the kid's room, the upstairs main balcony, the side balcony and even from the downstairs dining room. He cleared out some of the tree branches and bushes to make sure that the view was accessible from the downstairs lounge. To cut a long story short, this view became visible from almost every major part of the house. Anywhere you went around this house, you had the money shot. What did this mean? It meant that he had accentuated the number one feature of his already beautiful, stunning home. Now, this focus on the killer view was not the best improvement that he actually made to the property. His renovation was far-reaching and touched almost every aspect of the property and its functionality; he had actually changed almost every single aspect of the property to improve its value and utility. There was the fact that the electricity system had been upgraded, the electric heating had been replaced with central gas heating in banks so that the house would never be without water, the fact that that there was underfloor heating to warm the tiles in winter months, that the tree surgery meant that there was much more light coming into the house as a result of the culling of bushes and tree branches, totally modernized bedrooms and renovated bathrooms which were probably worth more in terms of real-life utility than the sea view. But as a seasoned professional, he was also aware that the true benefit of many of these improvements would go totally unnoticed by the buyer, at least until he owned the property. These major changes and comforts may be seen as additional things, interesting features, and nice to have when viewing, whereas the number one thing that the average person looking for a stunning villa must have is the wow factor. As illogical as it seems; wow look at the pool, wow look at that marble or wow look at that incredible view is usually worth more in terms of buyer hot buttons than wow did you know the central gas heating has six separate independent tanks meaning that if one part of the system goes down, you can just switch it over, so you never run out of hot water?

So in terms of utilising his Money shot, he did this by rendering the outside of the house completely until it literally looked new again, to give it that new-build look and feel as opposed to his neighbours whose properties which looked their age, and by making sure that you could see the villa's main selling point, its most attractive feature, which was this beautiful 'oh my god' view over the Mediterranean sea from every single location possible throughout the house.

Money shot executed. Cha-ching!!!!

Essential selling tool 2: Hot buttons

Brian Tracy tells a wonderful story of a salesman showing a property to a married couple where the wife had grown up in an area that had beautiful sycamore trees. This type of tree had a very strong emotional connection for her as she had always dreamed of owning a house with a tree like that in the garden. This story is told as a joke, but in fact, it is actually dead serious, and with it, Brian Tracey makes a key sales point. As the story goes, the house on sale had just such a tree within its boundaries, and every single time the husband pointed out something wrong with the house, the salesman returned the buying wife's attention to the beautiful sycamore tree and evoked those emotional connections, attachments, and her long-held dream of having a home with one like it. The salesman mentioned things that related to the Sycamore tree, which reminded her of her childhood and the happy feelings she felt in the area she grew up, the promise she made to herself about the home that she would one day have and the feelings which it evoked which she wanted to share and propagate to her children. And although not in the story as told, if he was a good salesman, he would have seized on her train of thought, agreeing that he understood the joys of her growing up close to her family and the wonderful experiences she had as a child, which the tree reminded her of emphasizing the potential of recreating that environment again, for her family, here in this house with this tree. Obviously, no matter what the husband said against the house, it was to no avail. They bought the house because his minor negative issues were not more powerful than the happiness and contentment the tree represented to his wife. The Tree was her 'Hot Button.'

Finding your buyers hot button can be just as simple as asking them exactly what they really, really want. (The song in my head has now changed from Pussycat dolls to a Spice girls single, somebody change the DJ soon, please). Unfortunately, because we live in a world where so many people are trying to scam you, con you or trick you, most people are very guarded and defensive, so they won't actually tell you what they really want for fear of you using it against them. These types of people will require you to pay close attention to the aspects of your property which interests them the most. This will give you an idea of what is most important to them, and you should follow their interest with a few open-ended questions to dig a little deeper as to why this aspect of the property is so important.

For example, comments about the size of the fourth bedroom for a family of three might be your chance to ask, 'Did you say that there were just the three of you, how were you planning to use the 4th bedroom, as an office space or home gym perhaps?' If they let their guard down, they may tell you that they have an elderly parent who they were hoping to move in with them in the future. Great, now you have your Hot Button, you can not only tell them the story of when your mother in law came to stay and how comfortable she was in that room, but you can now also point out all of the other aspects of your home that are also perfectly suitable for an elderly relative.

Luckily, not all people are as jaded, and some will actually tell you what's really most important to them when you ask. When I am qualifying potential clients interested in buying a house, I will often ask them 'what's most important to you, sea view or walking distance to the beach,' explaining to them that unless they want to live on a 90-degree hill, they can't have both so if they want walking distance to the beach they do not normally get a great panoramic view of the sea. So if their 'buying essential' is that amazing panoramic sea view, then they will have to be far enough away from the sea In order to get that perspective. I ask my clients these qualifying questions and explain the tradeoffs before they come out to view any properties and, more importantly, before I go looking for properties for them. I do this so that I don't waste my time finding them properties within a five-minute walk to the sea when what they really want is a property that has a view of the sea, the bay and the surrounding town and mountains, which would be impossible to get within a short minute walk to the actual beach itself.

So ask your potential buyer the question, 'what is the number one thing that's important to you with regards to buying a property?' And if your house happens to have that thing, don't be shy in reminding them subtly that your house fits the bill. I know I joked about it before but don't hammer them over the head with how perfect your property is for their needs. Think of their hot button like a doorbell; pushing the button intermittently as a reminder that you are still there waiting is not the same as pressing it in and keeping your finger on it until it becomes a nonstop annoying and impatient ring. Two or three gentle reminders, while they're looking around your property, should do the trick and at least one parting shot before they leave to remind them of the key aspect of your property which meets their needs can never hurt.

If their number one thing is to be closer to a school, try to work the fact that you are close to the local primary school into the conversation two or three different times. First, drop it like an anvil, so there is no mistaking it,

'Well, we are just three minutes walk from the school here.'

Then drop it more subtly,

'Well, a lot of my neighbours kids come home for lunch because they're so close to the school, it's great because it saves them money to give their kids lunch at home rather than give them lunch money for school plus they can control what they eat so their kids grow up with a healthy diet.'

Then drop it a third time later,

'This area is very quiet; the only time it gets busy is with the school run in the morning, but once that has finished, it's actually a very quiet area indeed.'

And then again, finally, as they leave, they mention how annoying the drive to find you was,

'Yes, I find driving frustrating as well; the best thing about us being so close to the school is that we never had to drive through and get caught in traffic; we just walked our kids there. Oh well, I hope that you have a more pleasant drive back.'

These are just a few subtle ways to remind them of the fact that their number one focus, which is to be close to the junior school, is actually resolved by the property you offering them.

Obviously, it doesn't have to be in proximity to a school; their number one want or objective could be a beautiful view or a large terrace. So as part of your small talk, when they walk into your property, you should ask them the most important aspect which they were looking for. Luckily for you, they said a large outside space, so when they walk onto your large terrace after having told you that this was the number one thing which they wanted, do you just stay quiet and let it sell itself? Not a chance, you promote it for everything it's worth, subtly pushing every advantage of a large terrace you know about.

Certainly, when they arrive on your balcony area, you will be able to see that they are impressed by their expressions, so don't boast about it, be cavalier when you mention it.

'As you can see, because it's a roof terrace, this terrace is actually the full size of the apartment. That's 69 square meters just for the terrace, which means that we actually have a lot of space and can do a lot up here.'

Then later on, maybe use as an example such as;

'Well, in the summer, because we have so much space up here, we've actually put up a curtain rail over that direction to let the kids have their own area and do their own thing while the adults stay over here by the beer fridge haha. Plus, we use that corner for the barbecue, and that area is where we had the Jacuzzi.'

This might be the second time you explained the benefits of your large outside space. The last time you push this hot button, and this will normally be the case, is when they ask you how much extra they will need to pay for the additional outside space in terms of government property taxes and community fees. In answering, you might say,

'Well, the community fees are a little bit high, but that's simply because we have a 70 square meter terrace which is more than double the space our neighbours have. As you know, the terrace is included in the price, but you will pay just a little bit more in government taxes and community fees because they are based on square footage, and we have more. So obviously, all of our neighbours who have a 12 square meter balcony pay less, but as we have the full footprint of the house for our terrace area, we've been happy to pay a little bit more. The good thing is that the terrace size is also reflected in the valuation, so the bank will value the property higher and lend you more money to buy it.'

Never, ever miss a chance to promote your money shot or an opportunity to push the buyers' hot button (if your potential buyer is kind enough to offer it up to you). Now, I repeat, don't treat them like an idiot and bang on about it continuously; they will spot it and see that you are trying to manipulate them. In fact, even if you drop it subtly, they will know what you are doing; the difference is that by dropping it subtly, they won't mind because it will be a valid response to the questions asked or a valid contribution to the conversation.

If used effectively, you can promote your money shot or push their hot buttons whilst they learn something about the community fees payable on your huge sunroof, the traffic in the area near the school they want to be near to, how the killer sea view from your balcony differs between the summer and winter months or the workings and maintenance of your jaw-dropping infinity pool. But whilst learning this essential and useful information, you will have also highlighted the fact that the number one thing which they actually want, is luckily enough on offer to them in the form of your property for sale right under their nose and you just want to make sure that they don't miss it.

So push those hot buttons, push them subtly but push them often, and treat the money shot like the final free throw in an NBA championship match, never, ever miss the money shot.

Estate agent panic button strategy: Ask to speak to the buyer

If you have a client who comes from an estate agent, but the negotiation is not going well or has stalled, you might ask your real estate agent to speak directly with the buyers. I know that this is a curveball and in contradiction with some of the other points made in this book but in certain circumstances, it might be the only way to move forward. Now, as requests go, this will probably go down as well as a lead balloon (I've never understood that analogy. Shouldn't it be, go up as well as a lead balloon, anyways I digress).

This suggestion will not be well received; for obvious reasons, a lot of real estate agents will not actually want you to be in direct contact with the buyer. They are going to want to show your house, take the buyer away, and be the medium of communication between yourself and the buyer. The reason for this is simply that, as the professional (if they act professionally), they are really in a much better position to control the negotiation and all aspects of the sale, and as a good realtor, this is what they do.

No disrespect to you, but unless you've been in real estate yourself, you probably know as much about selling a property as I know about running a wind farm. Well, that's cool. You are not supposed to know this stuff. Everyone has a speciality, and real estate is your realtors' speciality; that's the benefit of having them. When doing their job properly, they are often actually protecting you from yourself. They know things that you don't know. They've seen buyers like these hundreds of times, and they are experienced in answering the questions and aligning their fears.

But like everything, there is a flip side.

Many years ago, when negotiating a deal for a portfolio of properties, the deal was ruined by a crooked estate agent whose main aim was to keep me away from the actual seller in order to maximize his profit from the deal. In trying to protect himself and earn an extra fee (extra money I would have gladly paid him, by the way, had he worked to complete the deal as hard as he did to protect himself), I found out that if I had been able to contact the seller personally, I would have been able to keep it afloat. After six months of negotiation with this realtor, I finally got in touch with the actual seller, and when I told him my situation, he said, 'If I had known this three months ago, I would have been happy to accommodate you, and we would have got this deal done. But because I'm only finding this information out now, I am sorry, but it's too late; I'm now at the end of my deadline, so I'm gonna have to pull the deal.'

This pretty much ruined me; I mean, I lost a lot of money. So what's the lesson here? The lesson here is you need to spend your time to find a good realtor (I know we've been over this before), but it's worth emphasising over and over again and knowing my personal experience; you can see why). You can't just go to the first guy on the block. You need recommendations; you need references. You need to trust them. This particular realtor was the new business partner of an agent I had previously and successfully done business with, so I was blinded by the edification given to him by his business partner and the fact that I had assumed this business partner had already vetted him for skullduggery, lies, manipulation, small-mindedness, short-termism and greed. So I trusted him only because he was recommended to me by somebody allowing him to literally ruin me financially and just move on. That's what happens if you put your trust in the hands of somebody who doesn't deserve it. This happens not only in real estate, but it also happens in building, it happens in car mechanics, it happens in holidays, just tune in to any of those 'rip-off Britain' style programmes, and you will see. You will see how clearly all kinds of people from all walks of life get cheated out of their hard-earned money. People trying to do anything from investing their money right through to having a patio extension done get completely ripped off, some of the time by people who have been recommended to them. So although you should always defer your real estate agent's expertise, you have to make sure that you can trust them before you even do that. And if that's not the case, or if you have reason to believe that something is not right, then you may need to tell them that you want to be in contact with the buyer so that you can help with the negotiation.

From a real estate agent's point, other than the fact that you might totally ruin everything (which is a huge and realistic risk for them), the benefit is that they get to keep you happy. Plus, the agreement you have signed with him should protect him if you try to cut him out of his commission and deal with the buyer directly. The benefit for you is that you can actually be involved in the situation and make sure that all of your genuine points are being passed over to the seller.

As a property consultant, I have on more than one occasion told the real estate agent something that they decided not to pass on to the seller, either because they thought they knew better or for their own nefarious means.

This is one of the reasons why our two-pronged strategy of using both a real estate agent and marketing property yourself is so powerful because this way you get to split test the results and see if you're getting closer to selling the property from your own means or via the real estate agent. You can start to get a feel of if your real estate agent is really performing in the way you want and telling your potential buyers the things you want them to know, or if they're not. And if they're not, then you will already have everything set up to either replace them or just use the platforms and mechanisms you have already built with the FSBO side of your property sale to divert your energies into selling it yourself.

The offer

So let's have a quick recap. You have now prepared your house for sale (House doctored your house), prepared yourself to sell your house (know why you are selling), prepared the support systems and processes that you will need to sell your house (created your own marketing and chosen an estate agent) and begun the process of showing your home to prospective buyers (touring your home to your estate agents clients and the buyers from your own marketing campaigns).

Now that you have completed all of this hard work, you will begin to receive the spoils, and this means interest in your property. But you have not sold your property just yet; there are just a few more stages of completing first. You see, before the sale of your property comes the offer to purchase it, and after the offer comes the negotiation to agree on the price.

Again, I'm not trying to turn you into a salesman, but I think that you need some basic principles of sales as you are engaged in what may be one of the most important sales of your life, so it is important for you to understand the steps.

The offer comes in two parts. From a sales perspective, the offer is what you are selling. The offer is effectively what you are offering to the potential buyer. Butchers offer meat; lawyers offer legal services; you get the picture? But there is more to it than that. The offer is the specific quality and quantity of your product, asset, good, or service that you are willing to sell for a given price and a given time.

So to keep with our examples, butchers sell meat, but for the weekend, PUOR Butchers are offering 25% off of all choice cuts. Lawyers sell legal services, but for the month of January, PUOR legal services are offering 10% off of all conveyance services, giving you your own dedicated Paralegal to progress your case and are partnering with Flex Gordo Digital Marketing Solutions to offer you a 25% reduction in the costs of your lead generation campaign. Get the picture?

So the offer includes the price of your home, duh, obviously! But the price does not have to be the entire offer. There are other things that you can throw into the offer to sweeten the deal.

So the offer is not just the price of your home but the price of your home plus anything that you can genuinely throw into the mix and give to the prospective buyer to make your property better value than the other comparable properties they have seen for sale.

A great offer will kill your comparables, leaving you standing alone in the Gladiators ring, the blood-soaked victor of the fight to the death to secure the sale awaiting the sign from your Caesar (your potential buyer). Having slain all of your competition with better offers, he stands laurel wreath on the head and gives you the thumbs up. As the crowd goes wild and you heave a weary sigh of relief, you survived the battle of the comparables and won. Yes, they were entertained.

So what can be used to sweeten your offer for sale?

If your home is near a golf course, are you able to negotiate six months of free golf for your buyer? Most buyers interested in golf front properties are either golfers themselves (unless they are training their wits and skills dodging unexpected and random Kato golf balls Inspector Clouseau style), and so it is reasonable to presume that people who you know would be interested in golf front properties would appreciate the membership of the local club as a buying 'Brucie bonus.'

So see if you can negotiate this for a price that still works in terms of the overall costs of your sale, and if the local golf club doesn't play ball (excuse the pun), try some other sports activity that's close by.

Do you have a gardener who regularly comes along to tidy your outside spaces? Are you able to make a deal with the gardener that you pay him upfront for six months of work on the house? If so, then you put this in there as part of the offer. As you already have a relationship with the gardener, you are best placed to get a discount on his services, and as you will be not only guaranteeing him to work by paying him in advance but introducing him to future buyers, this should get you a decent price reduction on six months of work paid upfront, which you can cost into the price of your property and offer up as a bonus which comes with the sale. If your property has a private pool, do the same thing with the pool maintenance company. Running costs are one of the major things which can tip the buyer's decision one way or another, so a reduction in running costs to start with will often tip the scales of the decision in your favour

When looking at exactly how to cost this in terms of your overall return from the sale, understand that this is just playing with numbers. Let me explain how this works for you. Six Month golf lessons or gardening and maintenance might cost you, for example, 1000 euros. But for the buyer, knowing that those things are handled and that she doesn't have to deal with them might be worth 5000 euros.

Most modern businesses and services essentially trade in the convenience of some sort. I am well aware that I could take a course and learn how to maintain my car, but the convenience of giving it to a mechanic, even for small jobs, far outweighs the cost to me, not just in money but hassle and time. Conversely, I have already told you the story about the guy who promised his wife a brand new kitchen and after receiving a number of quotes (being a piss poor businessman) and having no concept of the value of his time and quality of labour, decided that the quotes were too high and that he would fit it himself. I already mentioned that in his own words, it took him five years (on and off, I hope not in one go), but she did eventually get her new kitchen. What I neglected to add was that in her own words, yes, she eventually got it, but it was a bodge job, and nothing worked properly. This is the power of convenience (and in the last case common sense); anything that you can offer to take care of someone, any action on their to-do list that you can remove and do for them will be worth more in their eyes than its financial cost to you. To the buyer, the value of your offer will be the cost of the item (we have already explained that by using your relationships, you will get it cheaper than they can), plus the time you have saved them in not having to arrange it for themselves (particularly in a foreign country this time could be significant) plus the reduced hassle and stress of doing something new or even doing it at all. Do you now see how the things that you can add to the sales offer of your home can be far higher in value to your buyer than the actual cost to you?

So back to our example, the full price of the gardener to a new client would be 1350 euros, but by using your relationship with him and the fact that you are not only paying him in advance but introducing him to a new client, you secure his services for 1000 euros. Ok, so you've reduced your profit from the sale by 1000 euros, this might seem like a loss, but in actual fact, it is a gain. Your 1000 euro less in sales revenue has decreased the cost to your potential buyer of employing a gardener by 350 euros (full price would have been 1350, remember). In addition, you have saved her the stress and hassle of having to look for a gardener, advertise for a gardener, check through reviews online or get referrals and ask for references from their previous employers, all at a time when moving into a new home have given them a thousand other things to do which or your buyer could value up to 3500 euros.

OK, so you've lost money (the thousand euros you pay upfront to the gardener)and used it to provide more value to your buyer, meaning that effectively you will earn one thousand euros less from the sale, but this is not the end of the equation. A few of these deal sweeteners thrown in will tip the scale of your property when compared to the other similar or identical ones on your potential buyer's shortlist. I mean, think about it, if this one offer of finding a reliable recommended gardener and paying him upfront is worth 3500 euros to your potential buyer alone, then three similar offers make the value which you are offering in excess of over 10,000 euros (in terms of value-added to your property). Now suddenly, with these offers thrown in, your 100,000 euros apartment will actually only cost them 90,000 euros in real terms because of all of the bonuses thrown in.

Plus, people love bonuses; it's in human nature to gravitate to deals that give us something for nothing or at least something for less than its original value. So when your buyer goes home to discuss the top three properties they have seen on their viewing tour, provided that all three properties are similar enough, your bonuses will trump the others, securing you the sale. In addition, as your offer already includes so much value, they are less likely to ask you for a huge reduction in price.

So there you have it, you spent 3000 euros which must be taken as an additional cost of your sale, to add offers and bonuses to your sales offering. This 3000 euros in cost to you provided, let's say, 10,000 euros worth of value to the potential buyer, which is why he chose to buy your property instead of another comparable property on the same street. Your offer led to your property selling faster than comparables on the same street, which in itself will probably save you more money than you spent in terms of running costs, lost rentals, continual advertising costs, and cleaning. But just like your buyer, the reduction in human cost, such as your reduced worry, stress, and effort from a quick sale, far outweighs the 3000 euros you lost in providing the benefits in your offer. Add to this the additional benefits you gain; I mean, if you had not sweetened the deal, it might have taken you seven months longer to sell, eventually selling for 25% less than your asking price as a result of desperation and stress as a result of the lack of making the offer of your property better than your neighbours.

So having a great sales offer is a powerful sales trick, and with a bit of imagination, it is very easy to do. All you have to do is find something that the buyer will find attractive and that you can supply for cheaper than he can find it for himself, and straight away, you have a Win/Win.

This is the key to the offer, and as many things as you can add to the property offer over and above the sales price, especially if they are not of great cost to you, the more attractive the deal will be to the buyer. This will allow you to create something over and above all of your competitors and outdo all similar houses in a similar area.

Your home, the one that comes with a free golf membership, free maintenance, free gardening, and the next quarter's community fee paid upfront, is the obvious choice. Another great sweetener for a rental property is to pay for a years' worth of property management or key holding services. The investor buyer may eventually decide that they do not like the service from your current one and eventually change to contract his own but, you have given him a year to research it and find a good one rather than just another thing on his long hectic list of things to do post-completion.

If you are selling a summer rental property, offer the buyer your rental client list (GDPR regulations withstanding, I am guessing a simple email to confirm that your previous clients approve of being transferred to the new owner's database ratified by a simple opt-in process that will do, but do not take my word for it, seek legal advice). Getting the thing rented and producing an income is the biggest risk and challenge for investors buying a rental property, so when comparing three properties in the same area at roughly the same standard and budget, the one which comes with a list of repeat holidaymakers you can contact and offer next years' rentals or even better next years' rentals already booked in, will beat the competition hands down.

Offering the potential buyer your rental book list is an amazing and captivating offer, yet I see so few rental property sellers do it. If you've been renting the property and you have clients who come back every year, don't just tell potential buyers that the property rents well; tell them that you will hand over not only the rental agent but all of your private clients as well. This way, you've given them a direct leg up into having an active and working rental business when they buy your property because they won't have to start looking for rental clients from scratch. What would that be worth to them? Well, if it took you three or four years to build up the rental client database that you have right now, to go through a handful of maintenance people and a handful of management agents until you found the good ones that you are using now, surely that's easily got to be worth 5% of the property price in terms of value to a buyer and might just make your offer strong enough for them to pick your property over a similar property that they might even like a little bit more.

All big decisions are made between the head and the heart, and tight decisions are usually a battle between them. Improving the offer of your property appeals to the head. They might get a warm fuzzy feeling when they enter your rival's living room, but yours actually comes with a better deal overall. I mean, can they really turn down six months guaranteed rental, free membership to the local Padel club, and six months pre-paid pool maintenance for an almost identical property with better Feng shui. Well, some buyers will but take my word for it; most will not. If you were choosing shoes, then sure, most people would opt for the stylish and fashionable pair that makes them feel great over the sensible shoes at a similar price. But a high ticket item like a rental property is far too important for that. In buying a rental property, the head must be given as much say as the heart, and when it comes down to it, if there is a face-off, all advisers would tell your potential buyer that the head should win.

This is what a great offer does for you. It puts you in the lead in terms of what the head says about the competing properties that your buyer could buy. The aim here is to make your property the best overall deal.

The Negotiation

After the offer, which is your side of the sales negotiation process, comes the counter offer. Yep you have beaten your competition for now, but we have only just started the race, and failure in negotiation could cause you to fall at one of the hurdles or allowing your competitor to catch up and overtake you at the last stretch.

Once they have your fantastically attractive offer, most buyers will still want to negotiate. I refer you back to my comments on human nature and wanting something for nothing. Yes, even though they have already been offered something for nothing, their human nature will tell them to want more. This is why you do not give them your full offer at the outset. You release your offer in stages. This gradual release of your offer is a skill, and even those of us who practice it for a living still need to make sure that we get it right. Your initial offer has to stop them in their tracks, powerful enough to put your property at the top of their priority list in terms of bang for their buck but not include everything that you could, leaving you space to add more to the bargain to counter additional request for price reductions or the potential of your offer stack being matched by a competitor whose property they actually prefer.

Questions

By now, all salesmen worth their salt know that questions are not a bad thing; in fact, they are a great thing. Questions show interest, interest to know more, and people want more information if they are still thinking about making a decision. If they have already decided and the decision is no, then the questions will stop.

If they have any questions about specific aspects of your offer that you are not 100% sure of, tell them that you'll get back to them either directly if they came via your marketing or via the estate agent if they are his client.

If it's something about the community of owners or the car park that you don't actually know the answer to, don't wing it. Tell them that you have a lawyer and you will consult with her before you get back to them, and then make sure that you do. This is a powerful tool. It not only allows you to appear trustworthy (the fact that you haven't tried to bullshit or blag them just to get a sale), but it also gives you an opportunity and a reason to contact them again. This also works with real estate agents; for example, If the buyer asks you a question which the real estate agent doesn't know (well, why should they, it's not their property), and you don't know the answer either. If you are present at the time (although if you read the chapter on viewing, you should not be), do not try and go behind the real estate agent's back and get the buyer's details directly. This is a no-no, and the real estate agent, if he has any sense, will stop working with you immediately. What you need to do is promise the buyer that you will get that information to the real estate agent as soon as you can and that she will forward the information to them. This not only edifies your real estate agent, putting her in a better position with the buyer but again shows that you're honest and trustworthy not just to the real estate agent but to the buyer as well. Then you go and get that information to the real estate agent (or buyer if direct) as soon as possible. Make sure that you follow up with the estate agent to ensure that he makes the time and takes the effort to get this information to the buyer; believe it or not, some agents (especially if they have unilaterally decided that the buyer is not serious) won't bother and in their misguided assessment lose you a sale.

In sales, this type of follow-up, answering the buyer's questions correctly and promptly, is called ˊtouchpoint.ˊ Each time you have a legitimate reason to contact the potential buyer (not an annoying high-pressure sales call but contacting her to provide her with some information which she has requested), this is another touchpoint, and every touchpoint that is successfully completed builds a little bit more trust, adds a little bit more rapport and creates a little bit more interest and confidence which leads you a little closer to a sale.

I will say over and over in this book, nothing is guaranteed, but I can assure you that you are more likely to sell the property to somebody with whom you've had eight or nine touchpoints. Touchpoints such as two or three viewings, three or four questions answered, two or three emails exchanged between the estate agent and lawyer, etc. Once they have all the information they have requested, all of their questions are answered, and this process will create a feeling of familiarity and trust. They will now be much more likely to do business with you than somebody who walks through the door, walks around the property, doesn't ask any questions, gets no explanations, and walks out again. It is possible that the latter will miraculously surprise you with an offer to buy your property and at full price to boot, but it is highly unlikely. A more likely scenario is that a buyer who has experienced a number of touchpoints finally decides that they are confident and comfortable enough with the process and the players they have been in contact with, to buy.

This is why negotiation is so important. You need questions, you need to send more information, and you need to go back and forth trading off the price with offered benefits. You need all of these things not only for their benefits in their own right but the additional benefits of creating enough rapport, trust, and confidence with you, a complete stranger for the buyer to spend their money with you.

The Price and terms

So questions are the first part of the negotiation. The second part is actually negotiating the price and terms. This is so important that I decided to give it more space to really give you as much help with it as possible, and so we will break this down in the following chapter but to give you an insight, let's just say it might not contain the advice you are expecting. There was a book by a guy called James Altucher called 'Choose yourself' in which he points out that as a businessman, he is an awful negotiator, and it served him very well in life. Negotiation is not always about winning the battle; it is about winning the war or, even more importantly, winning the peace.

Your furniture

But before we tackle price and its place in the offer, a word about furniture;

I take no pleasure in telling you this, and I know I'm gonna upset some of you, but offering your furniture as a bonus that comes with your house is virtually worthless. Sure, you may have a few buyers who show an interest in your furniture when looking at your home, but in reality, 90% of the time, including the furniture as part of the property offer does not create the great incentive you hope.

Your furniture is worthless to a new buyer because most people who buy a house are already planning to furnish it. Yes, the fact that they no longer have to spend money furnishing the house is a bonus, but not as big a bonus as most people like to think. The only advantage it gives them is the ability to use the house in the short term and not have to furnish it right away. But trust me, refurnish it they will, which means that in the grand scheme of things, your expensive furniture is not the valuable bargaining chip many of you are hoping that it will be.

Going back to the doctrine of House doctoring (see what I did there) and de-cluttering, we will remember that everybody has different tastes. So even if you have the most tasteful furniture in the world, there is every probability that the new owner is going to want to replace a good proportion of it. This could be just because they have bad taste. It could be because they have a medical condition and need to change the arrangement of the house to accommodate their circumstances, such as buying a different type of size of the sofa, removing the dining table to make space for a wheelchair, and so on. It could be because you were using the property as a rental investment and they intend it for personal use; hence your 'IKEA everything' approach to furniture is too impersonal for their Spanish dream home, or it could be the opposite, and your fussy personalized furniture will not suit the rental clientele they intend for their new investment.

So knowing that the incumbent furniture really has no intrinsic worth, I tend to throw the furniture into the deal as a kind of last-minute sweetener. The point of this is that the furniture doesn't have a huge amount of value and thus is not an important enough aspect of the sale to swing it either way, but it's a great thing to add on as a 'nice to have' and so might push a sale that is on the fence over the top to the conclusion.

Your furniture (yes, your Louie the 14th high art décor living room design) is not going to be what your buyer bases their buying decision on. It is another thing to be added to the offer like the golf membership or the pre-paid gardener and probably less valuable than both of them.

But in terms of use, it will have the most impact if you throw the furniture in at the last minute saying, 'Well, I know you're not going to use all of the furniture, but I'll throw it in any way, just to save you the trouble of having to look for stuff before you can use the place. I'm willing to do it so that you can start using it right away. Will that get us over the hump and can we agree on a deal today?'

This has much more strategic value than saying that the house is being sold or furnished because, in all probability, unless it's being purchased as a rental property, they really won't care, and even if they care, they really won't care that much

When I teach property investment, and I talk about rentals, even though I tell my students that if a property comes furnished, they should absolutely buy the property exactly as it is and rent it out straight away until they start earning a war chest from which to do upgrades, renovations and refurbishing, nobody listens. Ego, preference, and the sheer fun of moulding their new purchase into their vision ensures that they never do. They still go ahead and replace at least half of the furniture anyway, so I know how little they value it.

So even though you spent 20,000 euros furnishing your two-bedroom apartment, because you went to the best (and woefully overpriced) furniture provider at the time and bought the best stuff at the highest price just because you were told that it was the best stuff and would get you a higher monthly rental price. Let's just get it straight and take it for me; that money is gone. If you get the value back for your property, it's great; if you make a profit when you sell a house, that's wonderful, but you're never gonna make a profit on the re-sale of your furniture. It is extremely unlikely, and if by any chance you do, please contact me and let me know how you did it so that I can advise my readers of how you performed this minor miracle in future editions of this book.

Trying to swing the sales negotiation in a direction that allows you to make a profit or even get the value back on the cost of your furniture, is in my opinion, a fool's errand because it stops you from achieving your primary aim, which is selling your house.

I have seen too many sellers lose perspective and get caught up in the loss they are making on their furnishing at a particular price, completely losing sight of the real issue, which is getting their house sold. Their aim should be to make a profit out of the house's capital gains, if not then getting the value out of their property and moving on to new pastures, or at the very least, getting out of the problems of ownership and moving on to a new stress-free debt-free life. And yet, they give up the potential of all of these options for a lost cause.

The way to look at your furniture is as a consumable, not an asset. If you've used the furniture, it's already given you all of the value that you paid for it, full stop. Don't try and get another penny out of it when you're selling on. And if you've got lots of furniture that had been used and abused, do not refurnish your property before you sell it because this will be a waste of money. All the property has to have is some kind of furniture in it to give an idea of how it has been used but leave it open enough to allow the buyer to visualize how they would like to use it. If you really want to house doctor it via staging your home so that it looks as glamorous as possible (which is

219

not a bad idea), then rent the furniture from a furniture rental company. Renting the furniture will be particularly useful because no one will be using it, it's just for show, so there will be no wear and tear on the items leased; it will just be there for the exact purpose of staging. For prospective buyers to get a feel of what the house could look like if they owned it and could afford to furnish it as nicely in their style, it will be there to allow the buyers to come in and see what the property can look like at its best.

And if by some miracle they really like the furniture and want to buy it furnished, then you can probably do a deal with a rental company to buy the furniture from them or something similar to sell the home as requested, but personally, if I were presented with that scenario, I would just ask the rental company who they bought the package from and tell the buyer where to get it.

Oh and if all else fails, clear all of your furniture out, employ some professional cleaners and show the property to the potential buyers unfurnished. Although rented showroom style furniture or your own pre-used furniture is best, showing a property empty does have the advantage of looking like one of the new build properties that they will have seen and, as such, is not a disastrous option. If they have seen a few properties for sale, yours will not be the only one that they see without furniture, so it will not detract from the potential sale as much as you might think, and at least they will see what they are really getting, a property for the price without the idea of furniture value distorting either the seller or buyer's expectations.

Your attitude

A part of your job is to show your property to potential buyers and, even more importantly, in negotiating the final sales price of your property, one thing has the potential to undo all of your hard work thus far, your attitude. Believe it or not, I have known buyers to walk away from properties because they didn't like the estate agent or owner, and as an estate agent, I have in the past done everything in my power to make sure that the seller was not present at any of the viewings for the simple fact that the seller's attitude and behaviour had proven in the past to affect potential buyers negatively and lost me the sale of the house.

Don't be that guy, don't be the seller who is so frustrated, aggrieved, desperate, or annoyed that you put the buyer off. After all, the economic collapse is not the buyer's fault; the fact that you are in negative equity because you didn't sell earlier is not something that the buyer did. The fact that you are fed up with people trampling through your home and not buying it because it is not suitable for them, well, the potential buyer isn't responsible for that either. But above all, your desperate need to sell, your frustration that the house has been on the market for longer than you wanted it to and the fact that your bills are piling up, this is most definitely not the buyer's responsibility, and pressuring her as a result of any of the negative realities which you may be facing is going to work against the potential of you making a sale.

So what should you do? Well, be a good informative seller. Build a good rapport with your potential buyers. Tell them the truth, talk up the good points of your property, accept the negatives and explain them away in terms of the overall increased value of the property once your offer, bonuses, and additions have been taken into account, or in terms of the actual price which you have set for the property and the value that they are getting from this very reasonable price.

This way, even with the negatives taken into account, you are still creating a frictionless selling process that is going to allow somebody to buy your property at the same price as a similar one without a frustrated and angry seller, who is now argumentative and difficult to deal with. Long before Internet Trolls, the concept of a Troll was someone who lived under a bridge or under the stairs and was mean, obstructive, and unhelpful to everyone who tried to pass. Some homeowners are Trolls, and you do not want to be one of them; it doesn't create a pleasant experience for the buyer, and in sales, we know that rapport has as much, or possibly even a bigger effect on selling something than its price or quality. So make sure that you are not the Troll, and even if you cannot have a great rapport with every potential buyer, don't alienate them with the bad attitude which you have developed due to the circumstances and situations you find yourself in which have nothing to do with them.

Also, make sure that your property has great rapport; you can do this by having your property plan ready, your sales strategy mapped out, your valuation report, and your responses to all of the negative aspects of your home (objections), ready for when they are mentioned. Your home viewing walk-through planned out, the interior and exterior of your house doctored (tidied up and arranged in a pleasant manner), and a knowledge of the property purchasing system to add to your buyer's feeling of dealing with professionals all the way through the process.

All of these things are part of the rapport-building process as much as the way that you behave when you meet an individual. The way they speak, their level of education, their attitude, their sense of humour all equally have an effect on how much you like them or want to do business with them. The internal and external appearance of your house, the information that you have available about it, your attitude with regards to accepting its criticisms and what's wrong with it, and where it sits in the market of comparables will have an effect on how much your buyer likes and wants to do business with you. It will also have an effect on how easily they will be willing to come to any sort of sales agreement because when it comes to negotiation, believe it or not; it is not just the lowest price that sells a house.

So as the seller of a house, you want all of the aspects which lead to a quick, easy, and higher-priced sale on your side. Obviously, this rapport building onslaught is what you chose the estate agent to do, but even though you have an estate agent and even if your estate agent is actually good at it (remember many estate agents are awful), if you really want your house sold, this is also something that you, yourself need to do.

Top Tips on Sales and negotiation

- Learn basic sales and Negotiation techniques
- Push your potential buyers 'Hot buttons'
- Emphasise your properties 'Money shot'
- Make an offer stack to outdo your competitors
- Encourage questions in negotiation
- Do not overvalue furniture or renovation in negotiations
- Keep a good attitude, remember your circumstance is not the potential buyers' fault

CHAPTER 10: YOUR SALES PRICE

PRICE

Okay, so let's talk about the elephant in the room, the price?

How should you price your property? Well, most people have the same simple plan, to price it as high as possible and get as much as they can get for it. Now theoretically, there is nothing wrong with that; I mean, that's the whole reason you're selling it, right? But there are other factors which unfortunately come into play, such as the question, how do you know how much you can get?

So In terms of trying to work out how much they can get for their property, the worst-case scenario, which I see every single day, particularly in Spain, is people who price their property based on what they themselves paid for it. They simply ignore current market conditions and put their property on the market for the same price which they bought it for. This is folly for a number of reasons.

Firstly the price of a property is a derivative of market conditions and the type of property it is. Market conditions include a whole host of factors that stimulate or subdue demand such as income, job security, scarcity, the interest rate, as well as societal factors which may increase need, such as the divorce rate or rate of migration.

Some people believe that for one reason or another, their particular property is exempt from these market forces (which is bizarre because the market forces at the time of purchase were the reasons for the original purchase price which they paid), but I promise you that in 99% of cases it is not. I graduated as an economist, and personally, I don't care what anybody says; market conditions affect the selling price of every single property; they just affect different types of properties in different ways. So if your property is what we call, in the super high end (priced in the multi-millions of euros), well we all know that at this end of the property spectrum, the buyers (rich people) have always got money and as such, your property is more likely to sell in a downturn. In fact, buyers at this end of the property scale usually earn money in a recession because as assets values decrease, they have surplus money which enables them to buy more assets and buy them for below their long-term value hence adding to their wealth base. But this still represents the fact that they are looking for a reduction in the price of the assets they buy to make them interested.

The reason these high-cost assets still sell is that, firstly, the high price reflects that the asset is in some way unique and, as such, more desirable in any market, good or bad. Your two-bed, two-bath apartment in a tourist area may be less unique by virtue of the two to three hundred other identical two-bed two-bath properties nearby.

Secondly, at a higher price, the percentage average market decrease represents a bigger saving in terms of cash for the buyer. Put simply, 10% reduction in the price of your 100,000 euros property is a saving of 10,000 euros, but the same 10% reduction on a 1 million euro villa is 100,000 euros which as a cash amount is a drastic difference even to a multi-millionaire, as such high-cost assets tend to have lower price reductions than their mid-priced compatriots so when the overall market has fallen by 10%, high valued assets may only have fallen by 5% or even less. So although still discounted, a smaller discount represents a greater difference in the overall price of the high-cost asset having the effect of still making the property more attractive, and the unique aspect of the asset means that the buyer in its price bracket will enter the market sooner rather than waiting to see how far the price falls, to avoid others who value it more highly, buying it halfway down its price fall before they get a chance to offer.

This might give some the impression that this side of the market is unaffected by the price, but in reality, even though this market sector will stagnate for less time, it is still being priced and sold to the beat of the market corrections drum. So if you have been busy watching 'Million-dollar listings' and thinking that just because you have a multi-million euro house, you don't need to pay attention to market forces, I would suggest that you were watching the program but not paying attention. In a capitalist economy, everything has to pay attention to market forces from million-dollar listings and camper vans.

If your property is of high value, you now have an understanding of your market as it relates to economic recession and price. For everyone else who is not dealing with that market, price is going to be a bigger factor because the less money your buyer has, the greater the extent to which the price of an item affects its value to them.

In a recession, market forces dictate how much money people have to spend and the confidence with which they spend it. Therefore based on the scarcity of money or their fear of uncertainty, these same market forces influence how much value a property represents to them. So the value of your property goes up and down, depending on what's happening in the market. In a booming market, your property has more value because the buyer will probably have his subsistence costs covered and therefore have money in excess, which is why he is in the market to buy things that bring him additional enjoyment and have the potential of adding to his future financial wealth and security. Conversely, in a recession, the buyer will be scared about protecting what he already has, wary about adding to his financial burden and unwilling to overstretch himself and risk his financial subsistence and stability. Yes, I know that Warren Buffett said, 'Be fearful when others are greedy and greedy when others are fearful.'

But that's kind of the point. He's Warren Buffett, and his unique investment style is what has made him one of the richest men in the world. He is not your average guy, but your potential buyer probably is. As you are probably not selling a super high-end property, your potential buyer is Mr. Average or maybe even Mr. Just Above Average, and with this comes average type behaviour following what the average guy would do, which is to be fearful when others are fearful and greedy when others are greedy. No matter how many times your Mr. (just above) or Average misses out on a golden opportunity due to fear of losing his money at the early adoption stage and jumping on the bandwagon right before the bubble bursts, he, like the millions of Average investors just like him, is unlikely to change and you and your property are probably not going to be the investment to change him.

As such, if you want to get his business, you are going to have to work with him and move your offering in the direction of his expectations.

So if in this part of the business cycle, in your part of the market sector, the value of your property has now gone down, its fall in price is not because of any change in your property, but because the value of your property to the buyer has gone down. Allow me to repeat the point to make sure it is absolutely clear. When we are talking about the value of your property, we're talking about how valuable it is to a buyer and if they are buying a second home or an overseas property, for most people this is a want and not a need, so the value of your property to a buyer reduces in times of recession and you need to be aware of this and find ways that you can counteract it or accept it.

One of the ways to counteract this, which we have already discussed, is to increase the offer value of your property so that it's not just about the property in terms of the price but it's about the other things that come with it.

What's more, if you can build a rapport with the buyer and show her how much joy the property has brought you, the wonderful family life that you've enjoyed whilst living there, the extra benefits of the location or the neighbours and the advantages it has given to your immediate and extended family, these are all ways of increasing the value of your property in the buyer's eyes to go with the other things that you have added to the offer, making the property purchase a better deal for the same price.

What you have to do is increase the value of the property in the eyes of the buyer. Some things can't be easily priced in terms of monetary value, so a story about your kindly next-door neighbour who always looks out for your property whilst you are away and used to bake cookies for your children whilst impromptu babysitting them for you when you were late home from work, is a value add not easily matched by the identical property down the road.

But these types of tactics can only affect things so far, and at the end of the day, at some point, your price negotiation will have to come down to dollars and cents (or, in our case, euros and centimos).

If you're in a recession, the first thing you need to do in understanding the value of your property is to do your own research. You need to do your own research and find out what other properties are selling for. You need to find out what similar properties are selling for right now. Not six months ago, not 12 months ago when prices were higher and definitely not when you bought it. The price that similar properties are being bought for right now has relevance to the real and current economic circumstances of the world. All other sales price statistics do not. So don't just ask real estate agents and try and get your value from them because, as I pointed out before, it's in their interest (particularly if they want your listing) to lie to you. Obviously, a good estate agent with no ulterior motive would have some good information, but even if you find one, don't rely solely on the information you get from them. In fact, if you're going to ask an estate agent, phone up and pretend to be a buyer, a property investor looking for a deal. That strategy is more likely to get you an accurate idea of the sales price your property will actually achieve.

Alternatively, you need to use the other mechanisms available to find out what similar properties have actually sold for in the last three to six months. You must definitely use whatever other tools are available to find out what people are actually paying for properties similar to yours. I repeat, do not just look at what other properties are listed on the market because that information will not help. You need to find out what they are actually sold for or what they are actually selling for.

So the recent sales price of comparables sold is your first port of call in deciding the price to ask for when pricing your house. This is more difficult than it may seem, particularly in countries like Spain, where it's hard to get accurate data of what has actually sold due to delays in land registry updates and a lack of online service providers with this kind of information. In the UK, this is now quite an easy process because many websites which scrape data from the UK land registry and present you with the actual sales price of properties by postcode exist. But like most things in Spain, these types of sites do not exist en mass, and unless you want to pay 19.20 euros per property to investigate (Spanish Land Registry Nota Simple price at the time of writing), this process is not as easy.

Hopefully, by the time this book is published, Spanish portals such Rightmove and Zoopla showing you Spanish property sold house prices within the last three months will be available (just kidding unless I delay its release until 2033). As soon as such a site appears, I promise I will add it to any new editions of this book right after I wear out the keys of my laptop searching it.

So, failing information from the Land Registry or Land Registry scraping websites, the next best opportunity is to look for what's on the market and be very realistic. If you are selling a property which you bought in a property boom, and the market has now plunged into recession, this will be a very painful task; I know, I've done it and just so that you know, I'm walking the walk not just talking the talk. Allow me to give you a personal experience from the great recession of 2008. In 2006 I bought a property for 220,000 euros. If I go into the real estate portals, I will always see two or three properties at that exact same 2006 purchase price of 220,000 euros, but this is unrealistic. These listings simply represent owners who have no debts against the property or no pressing need to sell and so can wait out the property cycle until prices increase again and they can sell for what they bought it for. But if you have a mortgage which you need to clear or have had a change in your circumstances and need to sell ASAP, then this strategy is not feasible for you. For you, the strategy taken by most of the sellers is, unfortunately, the one that you must adopt because the majority of these properties are selling for 150,000 euros which represents a loss of almost 100, 000 euros if they can sell at all. This is the current price that the market has dictated, and unless you have no pressing need to sell, you would be foolhardy to ignore it.

If you want to get a good idea of where to position yourself in the market, the best way to do this is to calculate the average cost of similar properties to yours, sometimes called the median value price of your competition. To do this, you will want to get yourself some kind of a spreadsheet and record the prices of a number of properties that are as similar to yours as you can possibly get, properties that are the exact same size, with the same number of rooms and in the same location, actually from the same road or urbanisation if possible and then calculate the median value of those properties. Once you have completed this task, you can then maybe go down the road or to the next urbanisation, again always keeping to properties which are roughly the same, roughly the same size, roughly the same amenities, roughly the same location, maybe half a mile walking distance from your house, collect all the prices of the properties as closely identical to yours as possible and get a median value of them as well.

How to calculate the median value

So, for example, if you collected the prices of 4 properties which are all almost identical to yours priced at 100,000, 120,000, 150,000 and 170,000 respectively, then the median value would be found by adding the prices of these four properties together (100,000 + 120,000 + 150,000 +170,000 =540,000) and then dividing this by the number of properties on your list (in this case 4) giving us the following;

(100,000 + 120,000 + 150,000 +170,000 =540,000)

Then

540000/4=135,000

So based on this median calculation, you should price your property at 135,000 euros, not at the lowest price but not at the highest price either and definitely not what you bought it for.

Now that you have a median value for property prices in your market, you are much better armed to price your property. You do not have to price your property at the exact median value (in our example, 135,000 euros), but armed with the information, knowing the fact that this is the median price of the comparable properties to yours, you will have the right starting point to price your property above or below this baseline number based on if your property is better or worse than the average, and of course the value of your offer.

If, and this is super important, this median value is well below what you can afford to sell your property for because based on this price, you will be in negative equity (negative equity, meaning that the outstanding mortgage left on the property is higher than the actual price you would receive from selling it). You will need a specialist solution such as our company to guide you through the potential solutions to that type of scenario.

But negative equity will only apply to a handful of property sellers; if your median value is more than your outstanding mortgage or you don't have a mortgage at all, then this is your great opportunity to work it out right now if you actually want to sell your home. Because if you're not willing to sell for that price, if you are able to sell your property for the median price of the comparables in your area, but you are not willing to do so, then don't put your property in the market. Don't put your property on the market, don't waste your time, please don't drag an estate agent into the mix and waste her time, don't invite buyers to view your home and then refuse their offers which are based on the median value for the area and waste their time. Find some other way to get benefit from your property such as renting it out or keeping it for family use, anything else but find some other way to get value out of it, because if the price of your property is based on anything else than a factor related to this baseline, you will probably have to wait until the property market recovers and goes back into a property boom before you can sell it.

Euro per meter squared

Another calculation often used to calculate and compare prices is the euro per meter squared. This is the process of calculating what each squared meter of your property is worth by dividing the price of the property by its size.

For example, a property priced at 270,000 euros which has 94m² of usable space, would be calculated as 270.000/94=2872.3m². This tells us that you are paying two thousand and eight hundred and seventy-two euros for every meter square of the space you are buying into. Hmm, this property must be in Marbella.

You can find lots of resources online which will give you the average euros per meter squared for your region or town. Once you have this, you can do this simple calculation on your own property and compare the euros per meter squared of the price which you want with the average. If your price is way above the average, you are going to need a good explanation to justify it. If it's way below the average, then unless you know clearly why it would be considered to be subpar, you may have undervalued it and could possibly even sell it for more.

More on price comparables

Just in case I have not said it before, (OK I know that I have), generally speaking, in the technological age, it's never been easier for a buyer to do comparables. This is why you must do price comparables on your property, and you must do them correctly

Gone are the days when your potential buyer didn't know that there is a property, just like yours, with the same amount of rooms and roughly the same square footage that also comes with a pool or is on a golf course or is walking distance to the school which they want the children to go to, just down the road, but as they didn't know it, they bought yours instead.

The internet has made research so much easier, and research can now be done at such speed that nowadays, with very little effort, you can get good solid information about pretty much anything. If you add to that the potential to get other people to do the research for you, what you end up with is a society where information is now readily available, and the lack of information is now much rarer than it was twenty years ago.

So don't rely on your buyer having a lack of information about his options; he doesn't. Nowadays, he would have to put more effort into having a lack of information (you know, not have a mobile phone or a computer or a TV, live out in the woods without an internet connection, wearing a tinfoil hat and all that malarkey) than he would into actually finding the information that is out there. As such, make sure that you have done the comparables research on your own property. Let's face it, you're going to be on the same websites, getting the same information as your buyer, but this doesn't mean that you have to put your price at the lowest. There's no reason to do that because the person who is selling for the lowest price is usually the person who is most desperate to sell, and they are not always the best people to compete with (even if you are desperate to sell as well).

There is a very strange twist of human psychology which means that when somebody sees a very low price or a price that seems too cheap, their first reaction is to wonder what is wrong with it. This means that most people are more likely to buy the average price thing than they are to buy the cheapest, especially if you can justify its average price by building an offer stack that puts more value, more bonuses, and more benefits, creating a greater overall offer than the other average priced ones. This is the way that you make the price of your property make sense, not only in terms of why it isn't competing with the cheapest but also why it is the one that should be chosen out of all of the other average priced comparables.

This is where you want to be with your property, the same price as everything else, just with more value, better marketing and a much better organized, seamless and frictionless purchase process for the buyer.

Even more on comparables

Another way of using the same comparables that your buyer will be using is to ask an estate agent what has sold recently, not just your selling agent but another estate agent. This is another item from the 'Captain Obvious' list, but although it's obvious, you would be surprised at how many sellers do not do it. I mentioned before that calling estate agents posing to be a buyer rather than a seller would give you a better chance of being told the real market value of your property and help you to formulate a realistic sales price. But you don't just need to know what price other properties sold for in order for you to know why.

Everybody in business knows that the most powerful tool you can have is to have a mentor or, at the very least, a business role model. In the selling of your property, your real estate agent really should be your mentor; she's the one who's done it a thousand times before, and so she's the one who should be there to give you the tough love and tell you what you need to do to sell. Unfortunately, since she's probably going to have a certain amount of fear in losing your business, not all real estate agents, particularly the ones who don't have the kind of cash flow to turn business down, are going to give you the tough love you need and act as a true mentor should.

But as we have spent so much time and energy selecting a good one, and as your estate agent is your partner in selling your property, let´s assume that she is a true professional and has overcome all of that. As such, she should have no problem with sending you the window cards of a handful of properties that have sold in your area for the price you want to sell for. This way, she doesn't have to be the one to tell you that the configuration of your living room is lacking, to get those horrid carvings off the wall, or that you need to open up your kitchen and make it look brighter. You can look at the properties that sold and work this out for yourself. This is a very small thing but can give you the 'Aha' moment that makes the difference between you selling or not selling.

But if your local estate agent is still too chicken to give you the truth, then you are going to need to find your role models elsewhere. There is very little point in trying to find your role models based on properties that are still on the market because there's no point in role modelling the property that's still up for sale, hasn't sold for nine months and isn't gonna sell for another nine. You want to role model that has already been successful in selling, role model what has sold, learn as much as you can from it and then make sure your property is similar to the quickest sellers in any way you can. Imitate the quickest sellers for the highest price; make your property as close to them in every way and do so quickly and cheaply as humanly possible.

So look on the websites of real estate agents who have properties in your area, specifically looking for the ones who leave properties that have sold onsite with a big red ´SOLD´ sign emblazoned across them as an incentive for new buyers to get off their ass and start buying through fear of missing out. If you find such a site click on properties that have sold in your area and see what price they actually sold for. Also, have a look at their specifications such as; the kitchen, the bathrooms, the lounge, the layouts and try to get a feeling of why they sold. This will help you to choose the price of your property or improve your property to fall in line with other properties which have sold for the price that you want or need.

Price and location

Ok, so every seller knows the price they want for their home, but can you make a list of things that justify your price?

When pricing your home, you will need to make such a list and have it ready in explanation of why, even though the price is higher, your home is worth more than the neighbours or why it is such a great bargain and cheap at a price.

This is the list of things that your buyer is going to look for when making their comparisons between your property and others, so you have to take this into consideration and be brutally honest with yourself about your property when setting the price you want for your home.

If you are struggling with being honest, get a third party who isn't afraid to be honest with you (no, not the estate agent who has a vested interest in blowing smoke up your ass), somebody independent who is willing and able to analyse all of the pros and cons of your property in order to set a fair and attractive price for your home.

So what factors should you include in your analysis?

Let's start with the obvious one—location or, as we say in property, location, location, location, so important they named it thrice.

This is the Holy Grail in terms of property value, and as ridiculous as it sounds can be the difference between a 25%

hike in price based on different sides of the road or, more specifically, in Spain orientations and views.

Let me give you a quick personal story that never ceases to make me smile. Before we relocated to Andalucía, we lived in a quite impressive four bedroom semi-detached Victorian house in the South of London. My six-year-old son loved that house; in fact, we took him with us the first time we viewed it, and for me personally, it was the sight of the four-year-old version of him, totally at home, running around the large kitchen area that led me to decide that this was the house for us.

He loved our South London semi-detached house so much that when I first told him (now aged six) that we were going to move into Spain, he said to me, "That's great!!! So we're going to pick this house up and move it to Spain, are we?" I had to explain to him that, sadly, that was not the case and that we could not just lift up our four bedroom semi-detached house and put it where we wanted to in Spain. We were actually going to move to Spain and down size to a two-bedroom apartment (which we already owned as part of our personal portfolio bought as a holiday rental for investment purposes long before we ever dreamed of moving to Spain).

The point that I am making is that we had uprooted ourselves to live in a much better location, that better location being in our eyes, Spain. Because we believed it was a better location than the UK, we were prepared to leave the four-bedroom semi-detached house which we loved, a house in which we were just about to convert the attic to create more room and increase the value of, we left this to move into a two-bedroom apartment which was OK but by no means as nice in terms of bricks and mortar as the house.

That's the power of location. People will be willing to downsize to live in the right place. So you have to be clear in your understanding of the fact that no matter how amazing your home is, it's only worth half of the value it would be if it were in a different place. The most amazing four-bedroom semi-detached house, with a beautiful exterior, amazing interior design and killer views, is only worth half the value in Barking than it would be if it were located in Kensington because Kensington is a more desirable area (rightly or wrongly) than Barking. The ultimate real estate investors training tool Monopoly is a great example of this, so feel free to Google a Monopoly board and be honest with yourself, is your home on the Old Kent Road or Mayfair? And obviously, this effect is not only true in the UK. Houses in the Bronx will be worth less than identical ones in Manhattan. Apartments in Calais will be worth less than identical ones in Paris. And most importantly to you, apartments in Puerto Banus will be worth twice the value of identical apartments in Torrevieja because rightly or wrongly, Puerto Banus is a more desirable area that than Torrevieja is.

Even within towns, there are some streets or areas which come at a premium and others as a deficit. Which part of town is your property? Is it from Uptown where the well to do live, all theatres, museums, mummy mummies, Chelsea wagons and posh coffee shops filled with bearded Baristas pouring tri milk organically sourced coffee bean lattes? Or is your property from the wrong side of the tracks where school kids walk past the drug addicts on their way to the 9th chicken shop on the road with no police presence. If you bought in the latter, you wouldn't be the first person to, and you will have to be realistic about what your part of Kensington means in terms of the kind of buyers it will attract and the budgets they will have to spend

The final aspect of location which affects your property price is its location within the urbanisation. Is it a penthouse with better views than the others? Is it a ground floor with more garden space than those above it? Is it an end of terrace unit or corner plot, giving it bigger rooms and a better vantage point? These are all legitimate reasons for your property to be priced a little bit higher than your neighbours. Where is it on the road? Too near to the dustbins lowers the price. Too close to the school and the associated noise lowers the price. Next door to the kebab shop, yes, you guessed it, lowers the price. Be realistic about these things. Acknowledge and accept the aspects of your property which will deter potential buyers and price accordingly. Don't just assume that just because the average price in your urbanisation is 200,000 euros, your mid-terrace, 1st-floor apartment with a view to the motorway set right above the municipal bins will be worth that median price.

Location Location, location does not just apply to which town you are in. It applies to everything about your property, from which part of town your urbanisation or street resides to where in the urbanisation your property sits, right down to what's next door and what orientation and view your property offers. So, remember the median price is only your baseline to give you a guide price, but it will be the idiosyncrasies and foibles of your area and property which will determine what the thing is eventually worth when compared to others.

Price and home maintenance

This is just another no brainer. How well maintained your house is will directly reflect what people are willing to pay for it. Obvious things such as brickwork which needs repairing, damp or subsidence are obviously things that are going to be taken off the press in terms of the cost of their repair because they lower the value of your house in terms of its comparables.

Why would somebody buy your house that needs 7000 euros worth of work to be done over a house that needs no repairs at all when they are both the same price? It would make absolutely no sense for a buyer to do so, and as such, they absolutely will not do it. So make sure that your house is well maintained. Firstly in terms of the comparables, your house needs to be at least as well maintained as the other similar properties on the market at the same price at the same time.

But if you really want to sell it, I mean if you really want to sell it fast. It needs to be better maintained than all of the others on the market at the same price at the same time.

Now maintenance by pure definition is only the continuation of the standard initially created. Maintenance by definition does not include or require additions or upgrades such as loft conversions, conservatories, glass curtains on terrace areas or new soundproofing windows. Just good maintenance of the property as it was constructed by the builder or delivered to you should be enough. So just maintain your property at a level that keeps it at the very least, on par with others your prospective buyers may be viewing in the market for the same price. Once you have achieved this basic parity, you can add other things on, such as upgrades and improvements, as additional offers to increase the value of your property at the same price or even increase the value enough to charge that little bit more and still have it sold over others simply because it now has more value for the same price or at least more in terms of value per square metre than its nearest rival.

As I will explain below, any kind of renovation you've done to your property must give the buyer more in value than the actual cost of the renovation, or it doesn't become an attractive offer. If the full price of the improvement is just added to the base cost of the house, then it no longer becomes a bonus or a benefit, It just becomes a higher price, and that buyer will compare your property with the renovation (which based on their needs is a nice addition but not essential) to another property that doesn't have the renovation but still has all the things they need, and they will buy that one because it's cheaper. This is an essential aspect of pricing your property properly, so I will explore it in greater depth below.

The value of Renovation

Before I continue, let me make a quick point on renovations with regards to comparables. I have seen a lot of sellers attempt to justify their sales price with stories of the renovations which they have done to the property over the years; well, allow me to introduce to you another rule of thumb, and I take no pleasure in telling you this. Just like your furnishings, unless you have specifically bought the property with a plan to renovate and sell it to a specific market, you are not going to get the full value for the renovations you have done to your property over the years.

A property developer will buy a property in need of renovation; he will buy it at a below market value price and renovate it in a professional way with a clear end-user (or avatar) to sell the finished product to. This is a business process, and yes, of course, these renovations are worth something. They are worth something because they are part of a structured business plan. The purchase price, renovation costs, project management, qualities, profit margin and probability of resale were all factored in at the start and calculated so that the renovations would add value to a property in need of it and then be sold to a specific buyer already looking for that end product. If this is what you have done, then this section does not apply to you, but if you had done this, then I very much doubt that you would be reading this book. If you are reading this book and wondering what the value of your renovations are worth, the chances are that you either did them yourself to a passable standard or got professionals in to do renovations for your own personal use and to match your own personal tastes. If you fall into either of the latter, then I am talking to you when I say do not try to get the full value back from the renovation projects associated with your house when you put it on the market for sale.

You may well know that your renovation has made your house a better quality property than some of your neighbours and think that this should be reflected in the price. Well, you are absolutely right, and it will be. But let me be very clear. It may not be reflected in the price to the extent that you think it should. My point is that just like your furnishings, the value of your renovation to your potential buyer may be much less than it is to you, the value that you put it on, or even what it actually cost you to do. One of the reasons for this is because the potential to a lot of people is better than the realisation. So a great example of this would be if they are looking at terraced houses which all have attics, and there are two houses on the same road, almost identical design but one with the attic already converted and the other unconverted with the potential to do so. The house with the attic already renovated will appeal to some buyers because they now have an extra room, and they don't have to do the work themselves. That said, you probably still won't get the full value of it because they will compare your fully renovated house to the one which has potential and think that although yours is perfect, it is also more expensive and has no opportunity to improve in the future and increase its value whereas the other property is cheaper and gives the opportunity to increase its value down the line. Of course, not every buyer will look at things like this, but you would be surprised how many of them do. So rather than charging them the full cost of the works which you have conducted on the property, in effect you have to give them a discount on the work to compensate for taking away the potential of them doing it themselves and increasing the value of the property later.

Alternatively, they may be a builder (trade), meaning that there's every possibility they will look at the additional price you put on your property for the post renovated attic house and think that you've asked for too much money for the renovation as they could have done it cheaper themselves.

Lastly, there is the issue of taste. We have already discussed that most people viewing your property have none, but a property which has had all of the potential renovated and refurbished out of it will be of less interest to novices (non-trade), who want the option of renovating it themselves, and since every human is individual, they might love the idea of a renovation but not like the way that you renovate it. Even if they would only prefer to have had a couple of things done differently, it will affect what they will be willing to pay as a final price. And since there are things that they would have done differently, they may eventually use your property as a blueprint of what can be done but ultimately decide that the better option to buy is the un-renovated one which they can then renovate in their own time to their own specifications and standards.

So as you can see, the actual work you've done to your house is a double-edged sword. There is no doubting the fact it makes your home more attractive than its competitors. But be careful not to overvalue the fact that you have had work done or even value it at the price that it costs you to do because that's not always the way it's going to be seen when you try to sell it to a potential buyer. You have to keep how they see things in mind because they're the ones buying it.

So heed my warning well, adjust your attitude to the glorious I did that, or even I paid for that to be done aspects of your property for sale. Think of the improvements not as something that makes your home better than others or in terms of what they cost and should be added to the price. The correct attitude to take is that you did the renovations to increase your comfort whilst using it (living in it or renting it). That was the value you received for doing the renovation, so in terms of wanting the full cost reflected in the resales price, sing like Elsa (the cartoon character), or Demi Lovato (the real person), in Frozen and just let it go

Truth be told, the value of your renovation should probably be added to the offer stack. Meaning that you don't say, 'This property is so much more expensive because it's been renovated.'

You go through the value of your property, showing why it's at least as comparable to the other similar properties on its un-renovated merits and then you throw in the renovation as an additional factor to seal the deal in an 'Oh by the way,' fashion.

Such as 'Yes, this is pretty much the same as your other favourite property, but If you consider the fact that it's already been renovated, you are actually getting more for your money, and as the work has already been done, it will cost you much less to make the small stylistic changes you may want to personalise it and make it your own.'

I hope that you appreciate why this is a much more useful approach than using your renovation to inform the buyer why your property should be 30% more expensive (because you've put on a conservatory, renovated the attic or put in glass curtains). You might know you're right, and you might know that this is true, but I almost guarantee you, she won't value the renovation at the same level you do, and definitely not for the same price that it cost.

So the key understanding is that the renovation is something that you might have needed to do, so you did it, whereas your renovation may not be something that they want to do, or it could be something that they might want to do but not necessarily need. If this is the case, that it is something that they might want to do (possibly in the future) but do not necessarily need, chances are they'll buy the cheaper property over yours, secure in the knowledge that it has the potential to do the renovation that you did, if and when they need it. The real key to getting the value of your renovation in the sales process is showing the buyer that you can get the post renovated property for more or less the same price as the pre-renovated one. Now rather than an increase in price, this becomes a huge key to your offer stack. Now you are offering them the best of both worlds. Your buyer gets the property that they need with the renovation that they might want to do at some point thrown in for free or for much less than it would cost them to do it themselves. Just like the basic maintenance of your property before putting it on the market for sale, this offer is also a no brainer.

That's the key to understanding the value of your renovation in the sales negotiation purchase process, and I have seen this point confused and misunderstood, leading to properties being stuck on the market for months and sometimes even years; it is so important I have taken great lengths and some repetition labouring it, to make sure that not only is the value of your renovation not confused with maintenance but you are reminded of its place in terms of price and value when you price your property and enter into the sales negotiation process.

Price and Surroundings:

If you remember, when I told you that we were migrating to Spain, my son thought that we were going to pick up our house and simply move it to another location (I know, it's so cute), anyway, although a personal memory for me, this not only shows the power of location, location, location, but it also points to the power of surroundings.

I want you to think back to when you were house hunting before you bought the house that you are now trying to sell. How many times did you find the perfect house but in the wrong area? And by this, I don't just mean the wrong postcode or town, but the actual physical location and its surroundings within your town of choice.

How many times did you find the perfect house but it was just too far from the local school to make the school run effective, or just too far from the shops to give you the security that your elderly mother will be able to get the groceries if you have a problem with your car? A house that was just too far from the beach to allow you to walk on the promenade every single day, which was an essential part of what you envisioned for your Spanish home dream, or was just too close to the main road that as much as you loved the house, the road noise and its associated dirt and fumes would be too detrimental for you to bear. Maybe it was just too close to a school, so although you absolutely love the house and you can walk straight to the beach every single day; you know that the noise from the school kids playing at recess would annoy you making it impossible for you to work from home or the children will be milling around in the streets after school, playing and making noise just is not the environment you wanted for your bachelor pad and would frustrate you or as you put it,

'Kill your vibes, maaan!!!!'

So asides from the actual location (town, postcode, beachfront, a mountain with views), the surroundings of your house are also super important. In my book 'How to buy a house in Spain,' I make the point, no, in fact, I labour the point (you may well think that I labour all of my points well yes I do, but I am not just filling up the pages, As Antony Robbins says, repetition is the mother of skill, so even if her other child is boredom I want to make sure that you do not miss some of the essential points in getting your property sold, so I repeat them in different ways and in different sections of the book. Oh, did I bore you into making a profit? You're welcome) that you have to do your whole buying process in two stages. In the first stage, you have to go to the area, and by area I mean the town, once you know the region you want to live in, for example, Malaga rather than Alicante, then go to the various towns in that region and choose the one that suits you best. Know the area and choose the area in the area that fits you, your current wants and your future potential. So even within Malaga, you might choose Mijas over Marbella and then even within Mijas, you might choose Riviera del sol as a town over La Cala de Mijas. Then once you know that you've got the area right, you can start looking for houses in that area that fit your circumstances, wants and lifestyle plans. So even now that you know you want to live in Riviera del sol, there's no point choosing a house in a part of it which means that you have to drive 15 minutes to the nearest park when you have young kids.

Similarly, if you want a house where you can walk to the beach, but when you get to the beach, it's a rocky beach that is going to be dangerous and uncomfortable for your elderly mother, then this property isn't going to fly. No buyer wants to find this out after they have spent the time looking for their perfect house and narrowed it down to two or three. After all that work, they won't want to find that although the area is great, the surroundings are not suitable.

So surroundings are absolutely key, and although you may think that selecting the suitable surroundings is the job of the prospective buyer, not you, the seller, you can still pay your part, and if you play it right, it will benefit you in the end.

What you want, are people who are looking for a house with the kind of surroundings and local area in which your house is for sale? Never try and convince anybody of the fact that your house suits them if it doesn't. This is what all old school 'shuck and jive' salesmen (also known as conman) try to do. This isn't the same as promoting the benefits of your home. The reality is, weighing up the balance of the surroundings of your home with regards to what they actually want and what they can get is for the buyer to do. Your job is, to tell the truth, but just in the way you would on a first date, always highlighting the best parts of what you have to offer and presenting the bright side.

So if you are next door to a school and there is a lot of noise from recess, tell them, don't try and lie about it, just say

'Well, of course, the kids come out, and they make noise at recess, but it only happens twice a day. My neighbour works from home, and she says it's actually a good thing because recess is only half an hour, and it allows her to set a specific time in the day when she takes a break from work. Just like the kids, she uses the recess time to get up from her desk and just like the kids doing recess stop working and exercise, so she stops work and goes for a walk or stands in the balcony watching the kids at play. She says that it's a very good relaxing opportunity for her and useful as it's regular, so it helps her form part of a routine, and when the kids go back inside to work, so does she.

If they are worried about the school making the roads busy, tell them the truth but present it in the best light. You might say

'Yes, there are a lot of parents around at the time of the school run, so it does make the road busy in the morning. But it's at 8 am because parents drop their children off on the way to work, so if you don't need to leave for work at that time (if either you leave earlier or you can leave later), then it really does not affect you.'

So tell the truth, give it a positive spin but tell the truth. Don't try and sell a house in the mountains to somebody whose Spanish dream is to live by the beach. In sales terminology, if you convince them to do this, they will get what is called 'buyer's remorse,' which is the feeling they get once they have been freed from your hypnotic trance like sales influence and realise that you have convinced to buy something that they did not actually want.

Even now short term minded salespeople think that they can sweet talk buyers into products and services that do not suit them because once the transaction is done (unless they paid by credit card), there won't be any time for buyer's remorse. Because once it's sold, they've made their money albeit unethically, there really is not much that the buyer can do about it, but selling property is different. If you sold them a house, the fact that the sale happens in stages would probably play out like this.

251

You use your Svengali-like sales wittery to convince a city-loving 20 something-year-old surfer dude to buy an old Finca six hours drive from the nearest beach. Clever you.

But, what will probably happen is that as a property transaction is done in stages, they will reserve your property and then go away. Away from your charms and power to convince them, then realising that they didn't really want a house in the mountains, you just talked them into it and, upon reflection, need to break the agreement to buy. The process of breaking a reservation contract and not going forward with the purchase might net you a few thousand euros by keeping their reservation fee but is just going to waste your time and add to the frustration and annoyance of selling your property in the long run.

As sellers, our job is to find the right buyer for our products, our services and err... our properties. We find the right buyer, and then we tell them all the reasons why it suits them perfectly, give them incentives to buy ours as opposed to others who are a good fit and then guide them through the process of making that decision by giving them confidence, factual information, trustworthiness, rapport and if we can, even a little humour. We do not try and sell them something they don't want, don't need, that doesn't suit them or won't work for them and their aims. This is why marketing is such an important part of this whole process because finding the person who wants to buy your property is half of the battle. That's why I said, when you decide to sell your property, you didn't become a seller of a home or a vendor of a property; you became a marketer, a salesman, an interior designer, a house doctor and a negotiator. These are the things that you really became when you put your house on the market for sale, and you will need to master at least a little bit of the art of each, if you are to achieve your goals.

Top Tips on Setting your Sales Price

- Use comparables (the sold or for sale price of other properties similar to yours)

- Use the Median value of other properties sold or for sale to set your price

- Use Euro per meter squared to set your price

- Location in terns of Region, Town and within the street or urbanisation will affect your price

- Do not overvalue renovations when setting your price

- Do not base your selling price on what you paid for it

- Even if you can mis sell your property, don't

CHAPTER 11: SELLING TO INVESTORS

Selling to investors is a specific circumstance and situation far and removed from a normal property sale.

I myself find it much harder to sell to lifestyle buyers than to investors because I started my business as a specialist investor property brokerage and deal sourcing service, so selling to investors is my specialty.

In order to sell to investors, you have to know what their motivations and incentives are; once you know them, you have to play to them, and you have to accentuate the fact that the property meets those needs.

The first thing you need to appreciate when selling to investors is that, just like anything else, there are different types of investors. Some investors are looking for something to buy and refurbish so that they can resell it in the short term (flip the property), some investors are looking for something to buy and renovate so that they can increase its value and keep ownership of it and then resell it in a number of years (renovate, hold for the long term and then sell for capital gains), and some investors are looking for a property that doesn't need any work to be done to it so that they can just buy it and rent it out straight away (rental income investors), many of whom want it to give them a rental income which is more than the mortgage costs, running costs and costs of ownership of the property (a passive income). Some focus on yield (the return on a property investment calculated by taking one years' annual income from the property expressed as a percentage of how much the property cost) or the ROCE (the return you receive on the actual cash amount you put into the property).

Many Investors want to use a combination of these strategies. For example, some will buy the property, refurbish it and, if possible, remortgage it so as to recoup all of the cash which they used in the initial purchase and renovation, and then rent it out for a lower yield, secure in the knowledge that they have their principal (initial cash investment) returned to them safe and sound in the bank.

When marketing or even when showing the property to an investor. You can just simply ask them what their plans are; they might tell you exactly what they want, but even if they are cagey, if you're paying attention to the questions that they ask, it will become clear to you, and from this, you can calculate which type of investor they are.

Based on which type of investor they are, the next things which should become clear to you is which property investing strategy they will most likely want to use or at least which primary and secondary strategies they may want to use on your property.

Once you know this, it will be a great help to you because it stops you from trying to sell the wrong thing. For example, you don't want to be promoting the fact that the rental market is stagnant in your area and how difficult your neighbours are finding it to rent their properties only to find out that your prospective buyer is a passive income investor. Similarly, highlighting the fact that properties generally do not sell very quickly in the area but instead tend to rent long term will not woo your buy and flip investor. Again it might be great that there are lots of profits to be had from the rental market, but the fact that the long term price increase in your area is stagnant will not help you with the investor who only uses one strategy, which is to buy and hold for capital gains then resell, as the fact that the market is stagnant in the long term will be a massive disincentive to them. In all of the above cases, you've just lost yourself a sale.

Truth be told, a good real estate agent or your personal marketing strategy should have filtered out the wrong type of buyers before they even got to your door, but if they have not, or the buyer is looking to use a mixed strategy, then knowing what they want and highlighting the true aspects of your property which give them that thing, is the way you want to go

So you need to ask them what they've been doing. Investors, by their very nature, will be cagey. So you can tell them the truth. Tell them that the reason you are asking is that you know a lot about the property market in your area, and you can help them by telling them if yours is suitable for the type of investment strategy they want to use. Mark my words, if a house seller tells a potential investment buyer these words, he will knock off his socks, and it will elicit one of two responses depending on the type of businessman your potential buyer is.

Some investor buyers will be wary because they were hoping that you knew nothing about property or the market in your area, and they were planning to take advantage of this to, as we not so politely say in property terms, 'take your pants down,' which means to pay you as little as possible thereby making themselves as much profit from the sale as possible. Well, if the investor buyer in your home is there with this intention, here's the good news. By telling an investor that you know about the market and will be able to tell him if your property is applicable to his investment strategy, you immediately get rid of those people. You can pull the wool over the eyes of someone with knowledge so exploitative investors will decide that your property is not for them and move on, which, as results go, is worth its weight in gold on its own. Just getting rid of the people who want to exploit you and rip you off is a win for you, so there really is no downside. But the plus side is the fact that the investor who's excited and interested in the fact that you know the market and that you can save him a lot of time in learning if this property is really suitable for him will engage with you in the spirit of cooperation, making the sale as easy as possible. Because he already had decided to pay you a fair price, a price which allows him to make enough profit from the deal but isn't necessarily based on the bragging rights of going down the pub and boasting to his investor friends of how much money he saved or worst still, that he ripped you off, bragging about how desperate you were or how stupid you were and simultaneously how clever he is. As this type of bravado is not part of the second investor buyers' business model, none of this will be relevant. He will want to create a win/win outcome where he gets the best price possible for the property in terms of it fulfilling his need (yield, ROCE, flip value, or long term capital gains potential), and you still get a good deal on your sales price in the bargain.

So, use this technique to get rid of the first type of investor and to build rapport with the second, because once he knows that you are there to help him achieve his goals, he is much more likely to engage with you and maybe even pay a little bit more to buy from you rather than having to deal with somebody who has no understanding of what he's trying to achieve and is working against him at every turn. Because in the long run, particularly in terms of time and money wasted on the sales process, the guy who doesn't know what he's trying to do, doesn't understand the investment and is working against him could add 3 to 5% to the actual buying costs of the property through their ignorance, obstruction and defensiveness alone. You, on the other hand, having demonstrated to him that you understand investors and that your property actually suits the type of investment he wants to do will save his time, money and make the whole process much more frictionless, and there is nothing a business wants more than a frictionless sale. It allows him to get access to the property ownership quickly, to start producing those returns immediately (which is a huge selling point) and also reduces his legal and mortgage brokerage fees, saving him money on the purchase process.

So, in terms of what investors want, here's a very quick breakdown. Obviously, they need to be getting a good deal, but the extent of the price reduction varies wildly depending on the investor's strategy. For example, somebody who is planning a long term property rental does not need a huge price reduction (although they will want some reduction in price to ensure that they have a large enough margin in equity to use in circumstances when economic changes lead to them requiring a little bit of financial security). So yes, most investors will need to have a margin on the property and not just for bragging rights, but I also know some great investors who will pay full price for a property because, for them, the price is not the important thing. What's important to them is the rental income and what they want is a provable fact that the strategy of extracting income from the property (over and above mortgage and other costs) is sustainable in the long term. If you can help them to examine this and show them that this is the case, then you will get the full price of your property. Similarly, in a depressed market and if you have priced your property realistically, a capital gains based investor will pay your full asking price once you can demonstrate to her that there will potentially be an uplift in the price of your property in the future.

This is something that we specialise in and have spent so much time perfecting that we can actually guarantee to get an offer for your home within a 14 day period, often having it sold within 30 days. As investors ourselves, we know how to tease out the real aims and needs from investor buyers, and once we know what they really want (what they really, really want!!!!, as the Spice Girls would say), we find a way to structure a deal that works for both them and the seller.

For Investors, rental returns are usually most important because a lot of investors are buying properties for rental, and even if they're not directly renting them, they will want to know that they have the ability to rent them as a safety net strategy if their primary strategy of buy, refurbish and resell doesn't work.

Next is saleability; after purchases for rental income, buy, refurbish and resell is a hugely popular strategy and has been since the dawn of property investment. What they want to see in your property is something that they can improve, something that will increase the price more than the cost of the improvement and allow them to sell for a profit. The difficulty with this is it needs a buoyant market or a very cheap property with a very obvious ability to renovate and improve the value in order to make this work. An example of this would be a very cheap property with planning permission already granted, which would allow them to maybe add an extra room to the house or property which has already been given permission to have the attic converted into an additional room.

This way, even in a recession, a developer can look at this type of property and understand that although the market prices are low, at the price it cost them, they can still renovate it, put it back on the market and sell it regardless of the economy. So even though there are fewer buyers available, you need the few buyers who are still available to see what you are offering as a great deal and gravitate towards it. It's a risky strategy, but most property investors will tell you, there will always be deals to do in any economy. Property investors don't take the recession off; they just look for deals that stack up, deals that work, deals that they are confident they will not lose money on, and deals that they are confident will make them a profit. You need to make sure that your property is that kind of deal, and if you do, you will get them to buy.

This is one of the reasons why having your property plan is so important because if you can show your investor that you know your property. You can show them that you fixed some problems. You can show them other problems that have not been fixable or places where the potential exists, such as converting the attic, which was beyond your budget or extending the conservatory, which needs planning permission. You can point out that last year your next-door neighbour renovated their attic, and your other neighbour, three doors down, had built a conservatory, so there's no reason that the local authority will not allow them to extend yours.

These are the kind of gems that investors are looking for because it allows them to buy your property now at the recession price, do the renovation work and sell it immediately. In fact, even if they can't sell it straight away, they can switch to a long term strategy, renovate it, rent it out in the medium term and once the recession is over, they can put the property back on the market for sale.

So selling to investors is a specialist area. You already know the basics (I have just outlined them to you in this chapter), but you may need to go and do some more research on your own if you really want to focus on this as your buyer market. This is a book about selling your property even in a recession, so I didn't want to make the whole thing about selling to investors when they're not your only market. Obviously, we specialise in selling properties to investors, and if you decide that this is the right way to go, we can get this done for you. Take my word for it, I promise you that having worked with real estate agents for 20 years (even knowing that a lot of investors go to real estate agents because they're the ones that have big billboards and offices), you do not want to focus your energy on a real estate agency when you're trying to sell your property to investors. You want to focus your efforts on working with a specialist deal sourcer and property investment company who understands the language of the investors and can package your property in a way to make it have maximum appeal to them.

Just by way of explanation. I did mention at the start of this chapter that I found it much harder to sell property to lifestyle buyers as end-users of the property than I do to sell the property to investors. I started my business in 2002, and I did not have a property viewing; I never took a bunch of keys and opened the door and showed a property to any buyer for that first four years I was in business. I made all my sales over the phone, and I did absolutely all my sales, based on the fact that the property deal was structured correctly, the details were accurate, and as we say in the business, the numbers stacked up. So once I'd done the area research, the property research, researched the renovation costs, renovation uplift and the mortgage costs, the absolute resales price, the rental yields and matched this to the right investors, it was just a matter of time before we got serious interest. Our investors had all been pre-qualified and pre-approved for finance along with having had completed the reservation document that was sent to them by email and paid the reservation fees direct to their solicitor's client account ready for use when the right deal appeared, meaning that they could see the details of your property and have in reserve within the hour all done without having them or multiple others trape through your home repeatedly disturbing and inconveniencing you. That is the difference between investor buyers and real estate based lifestyle buyers.

When others talk about marketing a home for sale, they are usually talking about marketing it to anybody. I have pointed out that you need to know your market and be much more specific. Selling to investors, although a specialist market, can be the best option for home sellers, especially in times of recession because economic circumstances will depress the property market leading to lower buyer demand, reductions in market prices and fewer buyers in the market. In this type of market, selling to investors could be the lifeline you have been looking for because for them, the depressed market will not be a disincentive; in fact, it may actually be the incentive that they have been looking for to expand their portfolio.

I've been selling to property investors since the start of my property career. I found it much harder to sell to lifestyle buyers who wanted a home for personal home use than to sell to investors looking for rental income, resales profits or yields. You need to know an investors' motivation; his motivation can be uncovered by learning his property investment strategy but keep in mind to be realistic about your asking price because, in order to have the financial security to buy, the investor must have a financial safety net of equity in the deal. So regardless of their other motivations, one of their considerations will always be price.

Top Tips on selling to Investors

- Learn the different property strategies which property investors use

- Question the investor to see what strategy he wants to use

- If your property fits their strategy, sell it for all its worth

- Get a professional property investment company (not a lawyer), to help you structure creative property   deals

CHAPTER 12: LIES, TRICKS AND SCAMS WHILE SELLING YOUR PROPERTY

Admittedly there are always ways that somebody can trick you or try to scam you, but if you are the seller of the property, the probability of being the victim of a con related to your property is much less likely.

The main reason for this is because when you are selling your property, you are the person in control of the asset. So since the asset is yours, it's far harder for them to take it away from you with a scam, especially if you follow our advice and always work with a lawyer who will give you legal advice regarding the selling process and the laws that affect the way that properties in Spain have to be bought.

Also, as all property in Spain has to be bought through a public notary, the conman and scam artist would have to not only trick you, the seller and your honest as the day in a long estate agent, but also fool the Public Notary. Not to say that this is impossible but as the Public Notary usually studies for seven years in order to achieve their highly prestigious role, although it might be possible to trick or even corrupt one, the probability of being unlucky with this regard is reduced drastically.

But nevertheless, anywhere there's money to be found, there will be somebody willing to try and trick you out of it. So, here are a few scams you should look out for when selling your Spanish property.

Boiling you slowly aka Tenderise the meat

The main scam is endemic in estate agencies and something that estate agents used to do a lot in the UK. This scam is not illegal per se but definitely, a practice which is a premeditated strategy to force you to sell your property for less than you wanted, benefiting themselves and their buyers to your detriment. In this scam, the estate agent will take your property on their books at a high price, a price that they know is too high for the market and a price which they know that it will never sell for. (This is why doing the research and getting your own valuation so that you have a realistic idea of your properties market price is essential.) They will then waste your time with a handful of potential buyers who come to view, but because the price is too high, talk down your property, pointing out all of its faults and reasons which make it worth less than the money you asked for it. So, they put the property on the market for a while, present you with a couple of buyers who don't buy, frustrate and disappoint you and then after you've been disappointed a few times (believe it or not, it's only human nature to get frustrated and want to complete on a sale and psychological research has proven that this constant disappointment creates lower expectations), you've effectively been softened up to accept the low offer.

Think Daniel Day Lewis in his iconic role as William Cutting in the gangs of New York kneeling over a knife wounded Leonardo Dicaprio splayed out on the table announcing to the crowd

'This is fresh meat. Shall we tenderise this meat!!!!!'

As he slams his meat cleavers into the table before head butting you into submission.

Yes, in this analogy, you are the wounded Dicaprio stabbed by the lightning-fast butcher (an estate agent who is about to butcher your chances of getting a reasonable price for your property) about to be further brutalized before he finishes you off and sells your property for nothing.

And then, after you've been disappointed on numerous occasions and they know you're desperate to sell, they will step in with fortuitous life-saving occurrence in the form of an investor they know who is looking for a property in your postcode to buy quickly and for cash if you reduce the price. Now that you've been softened up to accept the low offer, they will swoop in with this investor who can buy the property but only at a greatly discounted price. He's a good guy, they know, and he isn't messing around; he's a cash buyer and can complete very quickly. How convenient…

'What will it be then? Rib or chop? Loin or shank?' he screams as his meat cleaver summersaults in the air, landing on the table just shy of your temple.

Obviously, they had this investor friend waiting in the wings all along whilst they slowly turned the heat up on you through a string of failed viewings and comments about your property being overpriced, and then just like the frog who would have jumped out if placed in boiling water but boiled as the water was heated slowly; you who would have rejected this investor's super-low offer outright when you first put your property on the market are now slowly boiled, worn down with regards to your patience, expectations and needs to accept. Desperate seller Frog legs can now be served.

So you are now faced with a dilemma. Do you really want your property sat on the market for another six months going through all the mental pain, stress and annoyance of all of the viewings and offers and deals falling through, especially if you're on a tight deadline such as needing to sell the property in order to leave the country or any of the other indicators of a distressed seller that you told your estate agent right at the beginning which caused them to hatch the plan?

They know you're within weeks of your deadline, and you really need this property sold when they miraculously present you with this cash buyer and based on the frustration, stress and worry you are now experiencing (pot boiling and your little frog legs are dangling), you capitulate and sell the property for 25%, sometimes even 40% less than you originally wanted for it.

Shouts can be heard from his property investor friends…

'The liver, the tongue, the kidneys, the heart!!!'

'The heart,' screams your William Cutting, aka your estate agent, the Butcher, 'this boy has no heart.'

And he's right; he has worn you down, frustrated you, disappointed you and tired you out until you have no fight left.

'He'll walk amongst you marked with shame, a freak worthy of Barnham's museum of wonders.'

And you will, you will be wandering around dazed and confused for years to come trying to work out how you came to sell your property for so little when others around you managed to sell identical properties for so much more

This is the real reason I say it's your estate agents job to sell your property, but it's your responsibility. If you put the whole responsibility on them, you allow them the power to manipulate your situation to their benefit.

Obviously, not all estate agents are going to do this because obviously, not all estate agents are crooks. But I've definitely seen this done, originally with property in the UK, but I've also seen it done a few times here in Spain as well.

The decoy

Another trick is for estate agents to use your property as a foil. What I mean by this is that they might have another property in the same urbanisation or at least in the same area as yours for which they have negotiated a higher commission. This is the property they want to sell to their potential buyer, not yours. So if you have been wondering why they are constantly bringing people around to see your property yet you get no offers, let me tell you the reason. The reason is that they never planned to sell your property in the first place. They took it on the books because they promised you a price which they were never going to get for you. They have a cheaper property or cheaper properties in the same urbanisation or area as your home, and they are using your property as a prop to sell them. In the game of good cop bad cop, your property plays the bad lieutenant.

This is the sales technique of showing the potential buyers three crap properties and then the one which they (the estate agent) want them to buy. They then show them another two or three unsuitable properties before they take them for a drink. At this drink, they allow the buyer to tell them which of the properties they have seen thus far they liked the best (believe it or not, nine times out of ten, they like the one which the estate agent wanted them to buy; uncanny, who would have guessed it). This leads to a second viewing on this preferred property (the one that the estate agent wanted them to buy right at the start), and some high pressure FOMO sales applied to convince them to reserve that property ASAP (I outline this strategy at length in my book, How to Buy a Property in Spain).

Believe it or not, in this scenario, your property is one of the three crap ones they show them in the morning in order to manoeuver them to where they want them to be. I'm not saying your property's crap. I'm saying that like anything, no matter how good it is, it is unsuitable for somebody. So if they're taking people around and doing constant viewings on your property without it resulting in any offers, you need to pay a lot of attention to the people walking through your door. Because if you can see that they're clearly not suitable, If they have young children, but you're selling a fifth-floor atico with no fences, and you know that it's not going to be a good idea to have a five-year-old running around the roof balcony, or if you've got a property on the third floor in an old-style apartment with no lifts and they keep bringing pensioners who are going to have trouble with the stairs to view it. These are all red flags that the estate agent is using your property as a foil to show potential buyers things that aren't suitable in an attempt to slowly but surely box them into liking and buying the property for which they get the highest commission. There may be a new build development property for which they will earn between seven and ten percent commission, and your contract with them might only pay five. This is a pretty good incentive to use your property to focus the buyers' attention on the new build which they want them to buy, so unless you like having your time wasted, you want to make sure that if you get the impression that this is what's going on, you take action immediately.

The fake advert

The last scam is possibly the most unfortunate one, and even worse, there really isn't a lot you can do about it.

Just like the fake holiday rental companies who advertise properties for rent that they do not own in order to scam holidaymakers out of their holiday rental deposits, there are crooks who take photographs of your apartment from your internet marketing and offer it out for sale at ridiculously low prices as a distressed sale caused by a family emergency (Catfish anyone). When potential buyers contact them, they tell them that the deal is going to go away in 48 hours, and they need to reserve it right away. If they create enough confidence over the phone (the reason they are called confidence tricksters or con men), the potential buyer will send them the reservation fee to make sure nobody else snares your amazing property at 35% below the true market value, and then after doing that a number of times and before they can be reported and held accountable for their actions, these people shut up shop and disappear with the buyers' reservation monies never to be seen again.

Now admittedly, this is not you getting robbed of your money, but it is still someone getting robbed for their money, so still sad even though you played no actual part in it. Worst still, I have known the original owners of the property to be contacted by the poor soul who has been robbed in this heartless way, desperately looking for someone to help them get his money back or to hold them accountable. This can cause them to try and embroil you, the genuine seller (who is, after all, just another victim) in the scenario, aiming to make you take responsibility for the scam even though it had nothing to do with you.

Well, what can you do about it? Pay attention to your online marketing and the marketing provided for you by your estate agent or digital marketers. Keep an eye on all of the portals where you know that your property will appear and if you see your property advertised elsewhere for a price that you know isn't yours, report it to whatever relevant authorities there might be.

This will keep your good name and your property from being dragged in the mud by these criminal companies who trick unsuspecting, gullible, and on occasion greedy potential buyers whose desperation or greed allow them to ignore the age-old adage of sales, 'If it seems too good to be true, it probably is.'

Top Tips to avoid Lies, tricks and scams while selling your property

- Beware of Estate agents softening you up for the kill

- Beware of your property being used as a prop to sell other properties

- Beware of online scammers using your property listing to scam others

CHAPTER 13: ONLINE ESTATE AGENTS: THE FUTURE IS NOW

If you are using the method of 'For sale by owner' aka FSBO, it's never been a better time. Online estate agencies have moved from being a small portion of the market to what is definitely going to become the dominant factor within the next decade. This can already be seen with the advent of UK companies such as Purple Bricks, who have no branches and use a mixture of outsourcing for listings and technology to list and sell your property, allowing them to charge a greatly reduced flat fee sales commission. The move from the traditional real estate model to this virtual listing and viewing was always going to happen, but the Coronavirus Pandemic of 2020 has sped this along rapidly. Due to the Covid 19 restrictions placed on society in most countries, estate agencies could not open their branches or conduct listings or viewings, but like all businesses needed to find a way to keep on working as best they could. This forced the profession to embrace the online estate agency model as they, like everybody else, were forced to move from the physical world to the virtual world in most aspects of life.

Change is almost always difficult and often painful, but in hindsight, most people will admit that the greater part of this discomfort was merely psychological as it is our resistance to change which causes more difficulty and distress than the change itself. Similarly, estate agents discovered that although many of the more established ones were extremely sceptical of embracing this new technology and way of doing things, adopting a staunch 'That will never work, real estate has to be done in person' attitude, most were surprised to discover that working in an online way was not as difficult as they had previously thought. Many estate agents facing financial doom if they could not open their doors and trade in the traditional way discovered that using virtual listing methods, virtual viewings (at least initially), along with other non-interpersonal working methods such as using Docusign to arrange contracts allowed them to continue working and minimise the detrimental effects that the Coronavirus Pandemic and its subsequent lockdowns had on their turnover.

By pivoting their traditional real estate agency to work as an online one, many of them not only avoided the catastrophic damage to their turnover, which they were expecting but also saw a massive saving in running costs.

It is this huge saving in running costs created by moving many estate agency functions online, which, when set against its minimal reduction in turnover, has caused many of these companies to now refocus their efforts into the online side of their business offerings. I mean, the forward-thinking ones knew that this type of change was coming; it was inevitable, but the Coronavirus restrictions gave them the push, forcing them to try it out, and its success has led them to embrace the future rather than have it drag them forwards kicking and screaming.

If you are following our strategy, which is to offer your property as for sale by owner as well as for sale by a real estate agent, then online real estate agents offer you the best of both worlds because you will still get the backing of a real estate agent, their infrastructure and business machine which may help you to find a buyer, but you also get the flexibility of probably being able to tour the property yourself. This means that you can arrange times for viewings to suit only two parties (yourself and the viewer), as opposed to having to factor in the agent's schedule as well. In fact, if you are very lucky, you may be able to do the viewings virtually, meaning that you do not need to synchronise with anyone else at all.

Now you know that our two-pronged approach to selling your home fast at the highest price advises that when working with a traditional real estate agency in a traditional way not to be present when they show your property to potential buyers and if you have to be there, to be like the old adage of little children 'barely seen and not heard,' unless questioned directly. We also suggest that you attend the viewing, which you generate yourself from your own marketing strategies and efforts (obviously, duh!!!!). The key downside of this is shown in the negotiation chapter of this book. When using a salesman, your goals and aims may differ from his, so although as a professional, he should, in theory, be better placed to convert a potential buyer into a confirmed one, this is not always the case. Even a good estate agent may struggle in closing the sale. Salesmen, like life, Forrest Gump are a box of chocolates; even once you've done your due diligence, you are still not guaranteed in terms of what you are going to get.

This is where using an online estate agency really comes into its own because not only do you get a reduced sales commission (this is not as important as they like to promote because paying less to sell your property is of no use to you if they take six months longer to sell it costing you money in additional running costs only for you have to relist it with a traditional one to get it sold) and their infrastructure but you get the ability to tour the property yourself meaning you get the opportunity to talk to the buyer yourself and if you follow the tips on sales and negotiation in this book, you will be able to close the deal based on exactly what you want not what the estate agent does. Phew, that was a long sentence; deep breath, ok.

So I reiterate, using an online estate agent who requires you to conduct the viewings gives you the opportunity to talk to the potential buyer, and if you've followed some of the advice in this book and maybe even done some additional training in sales and negotiation, you will find that you are better placed to negotiate the sale of your property than the real estate agent because you know your parameters, deal breakers, your real why (remember that chapter where we worked out why we really wanted to sell?), what you really want out of the deal and what really benefits you. So now, all you really have to do is to work out how much of that can work for your potential buyer. By using an online estate agency, you can do all of this without an estate agent in the middle acting as the salesman, conducting the viewing, making incorrect comments or unfounded promises and generally causing you any kind of problems.

So, look online at the offerings and opportunities presented by the online estate agencies which list properties in your area.

They may all work a bit differently, so take the time to read what they offer, then go to online comparison sites and read the reviews, Google them for negative reports and comments and don't forget to check them on the great unprovable claim and counterclaim social media platform in the sky, Facebook (just be aware that in exactly the same way some people post that they saw Elvis in their local chip shop last week. Not every complaint and claim on Facebook is valid or even made by someone we would conventionally call sane, so take all Facebook posts, good and bad, with a pinch of salt).

Find a reputable and trustworthy, effective online estate agency that works in the way you want to work and list your property with them to give yourself a third gun in your arsenal of the war to get your property sold quickly and for the highest price possible, even in a recession.

Future sale...Now

I'm only going to briefly mention this because I know that most of the people reading this book are doing so because they need to sell their house, walk away from the commitment and get every penny of equity or deposit that they put into the house out if possible. This is exactly what this book is here to help you do. But if all else fails, I would be remised if I did not mention the other opportunities and possibilities available to you in terms of achieving a sale.

These are as a group of property sales options collectively called 'creative property strategies' and are house selling tactics and techniques which we have specialised in for over 20 years.

As a seller, the ones that you will be concerned with the most will be the rent to buy contracts, exchange with a delayed completion, lease option agreements and owner finance agreements. Effectively, what these types of deals allow you to do is sell your house now but with the full and final completion at some time in the future.

What does that mean? Well, effectively, it means that we're breaking the sales process down into two or more parts. Currently, as the owner of the property, its bills, associated costs, maintenance and other responsibilities are all owned by you. If we break the sale down into two parts, you will see that you can pass the bills, mortgage, associated costs and even the maintenance of the property on to the potential buyers in the short term even though the title deed and ultimate responsibility of the property remain with you until the completion of the second part of the transaction in the long term.

So you will have abdicated most of the responsibilities associated with the property ownership for some of the sales price (either deposit or monthly payment), abdicating the remainder of the responsibility and collecting the final amount of the sales price at full and final completion some years in the future.

In terms of a 'Rent to Buy' contract, you will create a long term rental contract with a potential buyer who agrees to rent the property from you now, paying the rental fee every single month and having this amount deducted from the final sales price until he is ready or in a position to pay the balance of the sales price for the property and take full legal ownership of it.

This works well for buyers who have previously been renting their homes as rather than their rent continuing to be a dead cost to them, the rent paid to you comes off the eventual sales price, making every monthly rental instalment an investment in the future.

Example

A simple example would be a 10-year rent to buy on a property which you have for sale at 100,000 euros, where the tenant pays you 833.40 euros every single month. In this case, it is easy to see that after the first year, your tenant will have paid you 10,000 euros.

If your tenant continues to make these payments as per your agreement on the 10th year anniversary of your Rent to Buy agreement, he will have paid you the full 100,000 euros sales price for the house. So by using this method, you are getting your full sales price and all of your money, just not in a lump sum. If you are not in desperate need of the money, selling for full price via a rent to buy contract (100,000 euros over ten years) may be a better option than selling for below market value prices (for example, a 25% discount earning you 75,000 immediately).

We specialize in these types of contracts because they can create very effective win/win scenarios, but a word of warning. These contracts can be complicated, as can finding and vetting the right quality of tenant-buyer who would want to do them, which is why using a specialist to do this is advisable.

Lease options are very similar. They just have a different legal structure. With a lease option, you lease the property to the potential buyer with an agreement that he will purchase it for the agreed price at the end of the lease, so effectively, they are leasing it from you with an option to buy. So as you can see, rent to buys deals and lease options are by legal structure different, but conceptually they are pretty much the same.

The benefits of both of these systems are that they allow the buyer to effectively try before they buy so that they can be certain that the property, location, amenities and even neighbours are right for them before they make the full financial commitment. Whatever their plan for the property is, when they lease it or rent it, they can get to try it out, see if it works out, whether it's for holiday rentals or for personal use. Both systems also allow the potential buyer time to organise themselves and get their finances in place, particularly if they're not currently able to obtain a mortgage but plan to be able to obtain a mortgage in the future. There's really not a lot of difference between rent to buy and lease options; as I said, conceptually, the difference is just a few legal ramifications.

The concept of selling with a delayed completion is another very similar strategy where effectively you agree to the sale of the property to the buyer at a certain price but rather than the usual completion period (which in most cases is within a few months of the reservation being paid or at least two months or so after the exchange of contracts), you can actually delay the completion date of the purchase from anything to between a number of years to a number of decades.

Again, what this means is that you still have the full legal ownership of the property, but you give them the use of it. There are lots of reasons you might want to do this; there may be refurbishment work that needs to be completed on the property before they want to take ownership, such as would be the case in an assisted sale where somebody needs to do some work to the property in order to get the correct mortgageable value on it, so will exchange on the property to secure their ability to buy it, and then conduct the work needed to get the property to the value that they need. In such a case, you will enter into an agreement with them that allows them the legal rights and investor security to be able to fund the work needed on the property, and then once the work has been completed and the property can be mortgaged to the value required, they can pursue the sale as agreed.

These are all perfectly legal strategies for selling properties which are used by professional investors but in the same way that you see the warnings for TV programmes where people are doing martial arts or stunts, I strongly and very seriously suggest that you do not try these strategies on your home on your own.

Get in touch with a professional property Investment company like ours to help you with the financial, ethical and legal structure of these deals in order to protect yourself and make sure that they really are structures as a win/win deal, as opposed to an I win you lose deal. Working with a professional will create the security that allows you to be creative, think outside the box in your property sales and still be confident that you are getting the best possible outcome.

Top Tips on using Online estate agents

- Use online estate agents to get the best of both worlds

- Use online estate agents because they are cheaper than traditional estate agents

- Online estate agents also allow you to tour your property giving you greater control and rapport building opportunity

- Use creative property sales strategies but get a professional property sourcer (not a lawyer) to help you to do it safely

CHAPTER 14: THE LONG TERM BENEFITS OF THIS BOOK

So hopefully, by this point, you have completed the sale of your property. Congratulations. I'm sure you don't need me to tell you how to celebrate it. So now that you have finally got your property sold, there are other benefits that you will have earned from your time here.

So, what are the long term benefits of taking the time to sell your house right?

Well, the first one is you sell your house, and you get whatever it is that you want.

By now, you should have written down your primary aim for selling your property. If you remember, we wrote it down and the reasons that you're actually selling your home right at the start of this book. Whether it's money or freedom, security or change of scenery, stress relief, upgrading or downsizing, whatever that is, we have made a commitment to stay connected to our primary aim and make the deal that allowed us to achieve it.

The second benefit is what you have learned along the way. If you did this process correctly, you would now have learned a new set of skills. You know how to sell a house professionally. When most people sell their house, they are aware that it is not an activity they will do very often (the average person only sells a property three times in their lifetime), so they pay no attention to the process. They leave it all to luck or 100% to the real estate agent, and whether it sells or does not, whether it takes a long time or short time, whether they get their full asking price or take a huge hit on what they wanted to earn, they put the experience behind them and focus on what they wanted to achieve once the sale was made.

They forget what they learned along the way, which is a terrible waste of potential because, having completed the sale of your property, you now know how to sell a house. You now have a new skill to add to your skillset, and there are lots of things that you can do with the information you've learned here.

For example, you can add your new knowledge of sales, salesmanship, negotiation and stacking an offer to other aspects of your life. If you have a side hustle or a business, selling such a high ticket item as a property will have given you additional skills, which should make selling smaller products or services seem easy in comparison.

You now also have additional skills in marketing, and you can take these new skills and add them to whatever else you're doing. Maybe they will help you to get rid of the stuff you're selling on eBay or Etsy more easily, or maybe you could make a proposal to your Boss and run a campaign for your company leading to a promotion, raise or change in position.

Maybe there are elements of what you have learned which can now be used in your nine to five jobs, or if you do not already have one, you can add them to your resume and apply for work that now included knowledge of sales, negotiation and marketing. You may now use these additional skills to start a side hustle part-time business or an online business to supplement your income, and who knows, it might just grow enough to allow you to sack your boss and work for yourself full time.

But the absolute best thing to do with this skill, the most profitable way to use what you now have, is to use it to help others. Use what you have now learned from selling your home to help a friend, colleague or family member to sell theirs in their time of need. Use what you have learned in this book to sell another house, refining it and improving on it along the way. This doesn't mean that I think you should give up your job and go into real estate. What this means is that you can help other people who are trying to sell their homes, which is a wonderful thing to be able to do. You will be able to do this because you've actually practically gone through it.

And just like your real estate agent, if you can help somebody to sell their home, they should be happy to give you some form of remuneration once the sale has been completed.

Just imagine if you spent a little bit of time helping three or four people to sell their homes every single year and they gave you a small percentage of the sale price for the fact that you got their house sold for the price they required or within the time frame they needed it done. Imagine if they paid you that extra something that they were happy to pay in addition to whatever they are paying agents; you would have a lovely new additional stream of income which would not take up a huge amount of your time to earn because you would not need to learn anything, you would instead be using what you have already learned during this process and from following this book. And as with all of the best businesses, whilst you are earning an income, you would be providing a service that people not only need but are greatly appreciative of and are happy to pay for because its benefits far outweigh its price.

If using this knowledge to start a second income stream would be too time-consuming for you, then another option would be to make your money through referrals. Once you have sold your property, people in your circle will ask you for your advice when they need to sell theirs; some will even ask for your advice when they are looking to buy. In this instance, you could earn a very healthy second income which is 100% passive, by simply joining our partner referral program where you pass the potential buyer or seller to us, and we pay you a commission share on the completed sale. This is another option to make the most out of the experience of selling your home and what you have learned here but without having to put any effort in at all, just taking names (passing them along) and collecting cheques (well, we actually pay by bank transfer but you know what I mean).

Whatever you choose to do with the information in this book, I wish you the very best of luck with selling your home. If you've read this book and implemented the suggestions. I know you won't need it. What you have now learned through study and earned through experience is yours to keep, and I wish you the very best of luck however you choose to use the things which you have learned from this book to create a second income for your future.

Top Tips for the long term benefits of this book

- Do not forget the skills that you have learned in selling your property

- Use the skills that you learned selling your property elsewhere

- Use the new skills to get a raise at work, get a new job, create a side hustle, help others such as friends or family to sell property

- Use your new skills at selling property to become an introducer or an agent for PUOR Ltd. Email info@puor.co.uk for more details or google www.puor.co.uk or www.webuyhousesspain.com for more information.

SUMMARY

So there you have it, the complete Property Under One Roof (aka PUOR Ltd) system for getting your property sold even if the property market is in a recession. I sincerely hope that you have found this book both informative and useful.

I will repeat because repetition brings clarity. It's your estate agent's job to sell your property, but it's your responsibility to sell your property. You don't get to abdicate your responsibility because you have employed a real estate agent and then blame him when it doesn't sell. Because let's face it, writing a couple of snide remarks on Facebook and not giving him a recommendation is not going to mean a goddamn thing to him, but selling your property could mean everything to you. If you are not in the position to throw the money at it in terms of paying a real estate agent his commission upon sale, then you are going to have to dedicate some time to the crash course which I have given you in this book. In terms of for sale by owner, effectively, this book has been a crash course in real estate. The good thing for you is that it hasn't been a crash course in all real estate, just the aspects of real estate you will require to get your property sold. The sales plan, house doctoring, home improvements, sales strategies, negotiation tips and real estate strategies will have made you an expert in selling the one and only property which is important to you, yours.

You don't have to worry about selling a three million euro villa if you have a 95,000 euro apartment, and similarly, you don't have to worry about how to sell a 95,000 euro apartment if you have a three million euro villa for sale.

So this book will help you to sell your property without a real estate agent, but as you already know, I do not recommend this. Also, if you follow everything that I teach in this book, you will see that most of it could also be done without spending any money at all, but again, I would strongly advise against this also. Some people are obsessed with achieving every goal with zero expense, and in the business world, we have a special name for these people; we call them 'poor people' because, as the old saying goes, you have to speculate to accumulate. Approaching any project with this zero cost intent may make you rich in bragging rights, but a sober analysis of the true costs of doing everything yourself and the opportunity costs of having not used help allowing you to have completed it sooner will always show that rather than saving money your thriftiness actually cost you more.

Like most things, this is an issue of perspective, so if you want to save money, please allow me to finish the book by giving you mine. If you choose the strictly FSBO route meaning that you're going to save the 5% that you would have paid to a real estate agent to sell your property, you should at least be willing to spend half of what you would have paid a real estate agent (2.5%) to put into the cost of the FSBO strategies, tricks and tips that I gave you in this book. You will need money for the marketing, the advertising, the valuation, the snagging and the preparation of the house, aka House doctoring' of your home, before you market it for sale. You will need to make a budget for all of these things, which I have suggested if you expect them to work.

When selling your property, keep in mind the old saying, there's no such thing as a free lunch; everything costs you something.

As I said before, if you are in a position to list with a real estate agent, do so. The good thing is that you don't pay him any money unless he does his job, which is to sell your property. If you sell your property before he can sell it, then all it will cost you to list your property with him is your time, and you will have successfully maximized the profit from selling your property FSBO.

But what if you spent time and money marketing your property yourself and the real estate agent sells it anyway. Well, look at your personal efforts as a sort of a safety net, or as we say in the property game, 'belt and braces.' At least 30% of all agreed property sales fall through, so in this game, you really do need as many prospects as possible. Give yourself the added security of your own efforts as well as the real estate agents. Yes, your own efforts will cost you money in marketing costs, but it will double your chances of getting it sold, and for more so, this expenditure will be recouped. I've seen so many examples of someone who puts a property on the market with an agent and then abdicates all responsibility of selling it. After six months of not having it sold, six months of paying the mortgage, paying the community fees, the council taxes and often getting themselves in greater debt, they realise that all the money they spent on mortgages, community fees, service charges, government taxes, and the like could have been halved If they had just put that money into taking some responsibility themselves and making their own efforts to sell the property. They discover that by house doctoring it, making a home selling plan or marketing the property themselves, they would have spent less money but would have actually sold the property. So there's never a reason not to make your own efforts and do your own sales and marketing even if your property is listed with an estate agent, and that is the premise of the dual-pronged approach we have taken here.

You're not going to lose money; you just have to change the way you see the money which you have spent by understanding that you invested in buying your house, and now you need to invest in its sale. If you invest in selling your property by investing in a real estate agent as well as investing in improving it, organizing it and marketing it, then you are far more likely to get the result you want, but your overall expenditure will be the same because the money is going to come out of your account one way or another. It's either going to come out in marketing and sales costs which allow you to sell the property much more quickly, or it's going to come out of your accounts in additional running costs, bills, debts and potentially, fines that you will have to pay because your house took twice or even three times as long to sell than it could have.

I hope that this makes sense to you, and I sincerely hope that this book allows you to get your property sold, even in a recession, as quickly as possible and for the maximum price. I sincerely hope that this book helps you to avoid all of the heartache, frustration, stress, potential depression and financial ruin that having a property for sale on the market that doesn't sell can create. I've seen this on multiple occasions, having gone through three recessions in the property game, and of course, as somebody who specialises in discount properties and creative property strategies, these adverse circumstances can give us great deals.

But there is more to what I do than that. There is more to a great deal than the money we make out of it. I am well aware that some people think that we are just a bunch of harbour sharks looking for blood in the water and waiting to chew the 'victims' legs for our own profit. But what these people do not realise or want to see is that we provide a great service to people who are really in need to get rid of their properties, desperate to get out of the financial ruin and buckling under the strain of not being able to sell.

What we help them to do is accept the reality of their situation, discover what it is really worth in terms of their personal aims and goals to sell the property, advise them as to what their property is really worth in the current market, agree on a value that they can accept for its sale and then help them to sell it and move on with their lives. By doing this, we are helping them to avoid the stress and financial penalties of CCJ's, bankruptcy, social stigma and financial destitution. What the naysayers do not appreciate is that ninety percent of the time (myself included, bearing in mind that I lost 3 million pounds worth of property in the great recession of 2008), once you've got past the initial frustration of how much money you ideally wanted for the property, you soon realise that your sanity, mental health, physical health and overall well being is worth much more than the reduction in price, because, with those things intact, you can always rebuild your portfolio and get your financial wealth back. I should know I'm doing it right now.

So that is why I wrote this book. That is why I'm giving this information away. This is all the stuff I would use to help you to sell your property, and make thousands, sometimes tens of thousands of pounds in profit doing so. But I've learned over the years from my mentors that there is often a difference between knowledge and implementation.

I have now given you all the knowledge that I have; please go ahead and use it to the best of your ability, and I genuinely wish you all the success in the world. But if you are one of the people who, for one reason or another, would like some help with the implementation, well, that's where we come in. If you don't want to do it yourself, and you really need, for whatever reason, a done for you service, then please feel free to contact us. We will be more than happy to use all of the advice, suggestions, secrets, tricks and tips that we gave you in this book, applied and amplified by our 20 plus years of experience in the property industry, to get the job done for you and sell your property quickly for the maximum realistically attainable price regardless of the economic circumstances we find ourselves in.

Printed in Great Britain
by Amazon